Dark Secrets

Dark Secrets

August Alexander

ISBN:978-1-956736-79-3(Paperback Edition)
ISBN:978-1-956736-80-9(Hardcover Edition)
ISBN:978-1-956736-78-6(E-book Edition)

Some characters and events in this book are fictitious. Any similarity to the real persons, living or dead, is coincidental and not intended by the author.

Book Ordering Information

Phone Number: 315 288-7939 ext. 1000 or 347-901-4920
Email: info@globalsummithouse.com
Global Summit House
www.globalsummithouse.com

Printed in the United States of America

Contents

Dedication

This book is dedicated o my mom.
For whom without I would not be here doing what I love.

Life is like a puzzle. When it falls apart we must struggle to put the pieces back together again. Sometimes in life when we think that we know the truth it turns out that we actually know nothing and therefore we have to go back and find what we are missing.

Even if it means reliving the pain of our past or discovering something that we never would have thought existed. Sometimes life can be like one big dark secret and you have to find your way to the truth. It is only by finding the truth that you can find your way to the light.

Preface

As I held her body in my arms waiting for the ambulance to arrive I looked across the road to see a woman and a boy who looked to be my age staring back at me. The woman seemed to look at me with furious eyes. I guess that was because I was a vampire and my friend was a human.

I looked back down to check on my friend. When I looked up the woman and the boy were gone. It was as if they had vanished. Something inside of me was telling me that something was wrong. I knew that something was coming but I couldn't place my finger on what it was. Life as I knew it was about to become even more unbearable.

Chapter 1

Celebration

Star looked amazing in the lavender dress that she wore. Victor and Darren of course wore their black suits while Mason wore his usual style of blue jeans and buttoned up shirts.

Caleb and I however stuck to our simple sense of fashion. Caleb wore jeans and buttoned up jeans while I wore a simple long thin strapped red dress. Amelia wore long green dress. Green was Amelia's best color. It always went well with her flaming red hair. After the celebration was over we all headed back to our rooms to turn in before the sun came up.

We were planning to leave the next night and head toward Pensacola. The anniversary of my mother's death was coming up in a week and Alyssa and I wanted to go pay our respects but in all truth I wasn't sure if I was ready to go back there. I wasn't sure if I was ready to face the past again.

Just in the moment of that thought Amelia entered my room while I was waiting for Caleb. "You have got to go back and face the past sometime" Amelia said. I knew that it was digging around in my head now. " I knew Amelia but it's just hard." I replied. Amelia came to sit down on the bed beside me. "It's not easy being a vampire but we have to learn to adapt to it." Amelia said as she put her hand around me. "No it's not." I said as I laid my head on her shoulder.

"We are what we are Elizabeth." Amelia said as she ran her fingers through my hair. "I know I just don't think that I can handle going to my mother's grave." I told her. "I know how you feel." It's sad that your mother is gone but you have to move on." Amelia replied. "Your right Amelia. I have to face this." I said as I leaned forward to hug her. "That's right Amelia agreed.

"Thank you Amelia such a good friend." I looked up to see Caleb standing in the doorway. "Are you ready to turn in the night?" Caleb asked. "You have no idea." I replied. "Well good night you too." Amelia said. Darren entered the room as Amelia was getting ready to walk out. "Ready for bed babe?" Darren asked. "Yeah." Amelia replied. "Don't break the furniture this time." Darren teased. Amelia smacked Darren on the arm.

"At least someone is doing something constructive around here."

I said with a big smile on my face. "Funny. Darren replied. "What's the matter brother? Did I steal your thunder?" I asked with a big grin. "No." Darren said as he stomped off down the hall. "That was kind of funny." Amelia said. "No it wasn't! Darren yelled from down the hall. "Good night you too." Amelia said as she walk out of the room and closed the door. I laid on the bed feeling as if I was completely ran down. Caleb came over and laid beside me.

"You really don't want to go back to Pensacola do you?" Caleb asked." No watching my mother die was hard enough. I don't think that I can stand at her grave." I replied. " I know what you mean. I lost my mother when I was thirteen. "I turn my head toward Caleb and looked at him with remorse.

"What happened?" I asked. "My mother died of a severe plague. I was left to take care of my brother. My father had to work in order to provide for us. I raised my brothers up and took care of the land while we worked to support us. We didn't have any family left to take us in." Caleb explain "That must have been hard." I told him. "I t was even after father died I took care of my brothers. I couldn't abandon them "They were all I had left. Caleb said as tears of blood began to fall down his face. I took my hand and wipe the tears away as I kissed him. We continued to talk for a few minutes and then I fell asleep. The day passed rather quickly and before we knew it night had come again. We were scheduled to board our flight at nine o'clock.

I went to grab an ivory sweater and some jeans from the closet and headed toward the bathroom to take a shower. When I came out of the bathroom I started to pack some clothes while Caleb waited down stairs with the others. After a few minutes Alyssa came in to check on me. "Are you ready to go?" Alyssa asked. "As ready as I'll ever be. "I replied. "Elizabeth, I know that you are not happy about going back but sometimes we have to do things that we don't want to do."

I stopped packing my clothes and sat down on the bed. "I know I just didn't think that we would be going back so soon." I replied. I understand but we have to honor her memory. "She was our mother. "Alyssa said as she sat down on the bed beside me.

3 Weeks Later

" More memories. That's all a vampire seems to have other than time." I said in a sarcastic voice. "It never ends." I added. "I'm sorry Elizabeth, I didn't mean to upset you." Alyssa replied. "It's not you, I'm just upset with this whole situation." I explained. I got up off the bed and continued packing. I had to watch our mother die and that kind of tragedy sticks with you. "It never goes away. I said as I kept shoving clothes in the suitcase. "It's not your fault Elizabeth."

Isn't it?" I said. "If I had just told mom the truth and if I just gotten her out the house the first night I was there then she wouldn't have been there when Vladimir attacked. If I had done that then she would still be alive today." I said as I slammed the suitcase shut.

"You don't know that!" Alyssa snapped, An you do!" I snapped back. In that moment I realize that I was taking my anger on her. "I'm sorry for snapping." I told her. "Me too." Alyssa replied. We hugged each other and made up. After a moment Victor entered the room. He stood there in his jeans and black trench coat looking at us with a smile on his face. "Well look at who finally decided to kiss and make up." Victor teased. "Oh shut it Victor." Alyssa said. "Are you too ready to go yet?. Victor asked. "yeah we will be right down." I told him.

As Victor left he tapped Alyssa playfully on the head. "Hey!" Alyssa said laughing as she jumped on Victor's back and wrapped her arms around his neck. As Victor carried Alyssa downstairs I grabbed my suitcase and started to follow them. I stopped for a moment and thought how much I didn't want to do this but I know deep down that Amelia and Alyssa were right. I had to have the past again. The past would always be there and I knew I could ever escape from it.

When I got downstairs I saw everyone standing by the door waiting for me. "Let's go." I told them. We headed out the door and loaded up in our cars and headed up to the airport. I finally convinced Caleb to get a couple of cars. I knew that we didn't need them but it was nice to have them. even though we were faster than any human or vehicle.

I just wanted Caleb to get familiar with the modern technology. We had two black cars. They were Hondas of course. I love Hondas.

Alyssa and Mason rode with Caleb and I while Victor and Star rode with Amelia and Darren. When we got to go to the airport I began to have a lot of thoughts run through my mind. I could tell by the look on Amelia's face that she was digging around in my head again as I stood next to her while we waited in line at the gate. "How long are you going to keep doing that " I asked. I'm sorry. You just seem so sad. Amelia replied. "When are you going to stop blaming yourself for your mother's death and that you have family that cares about you?" Amelia asked.

"It was my fault." I replied. "No it wasn't. You can't keep blaming yourself Elizabeth." I turned around to face Amelia with a look of anger. "What if I don't want to?" What if I want to join her?" I said in a harsh voice. The others turned to look at us with a shock on their faces. Alyssa and Caleb looked more shocked than the others. Everyone remained silent except for Alyssa. "I can't believe that you would say that." Alyssa said in a harsh voice. "Don't we mean anything to you?" Amelia asked.

"Of course you do". I replied. "You all just don't understand what I'm going through." Don't I?"

Alyssa asked she was my mother too." I started feeling bad for saying that. I know that everyone understand was I was going through. I guess I just had one of my moments were I spoke without thinking. "Alyssa." Mason said he reached to grab her arm. "I didn't mean it that way. I'm just breaking apart I guess." I told them.

Alyssa came over to hug me. "I don't like this any better than you do but she was our mother. We owe it to her to go and pay our respects." Alyssa said. "Your right I'm sorry. Forgive me." I replied. "Of course" Amelia said. Amelia put her arm around me as we waited in line at the gate to board our flight. As I sat on the plane with the others I thought about my mother. I looked out in the window into the beauty of the night looking up at the moon. I tried to relax and just let everything go for a moment.

"Did you really mean what you said about wanting to join your mother?" Caleb asked." No I lied. "I was just upset." I added. "Besides, you know me better than that." Caleb looked at me as if he was unsure about something. "Do I?." Caleb asked because I'm not so sure anymore Elizabeth." Do I?" Caleb asked. "Because I'm not so sure anymore Elizabeth. I couldn't blame Caleb for saying that. Hell I was starting to agree with him. I wasn't sure I knew myself anymore. I felt like I was becoming completely different person.

"This whole thing is just really upsetting and really hard for me right now." I replied." "I know how you feel." Caleb said as he reached out to take my hand. "I lost my parents too." I started to feel like a big jerk for forgetting that Caleb has lost his parents. "I'm sorry." I'm just falling apart. "I told him. Caleb looked at me with his normal look of understanding.

"Well even though you may be falling apart you still look pretty damn good from where I'm setting." Caleb reassured me. I reached out and took Caleb's hand as I turned around to look back out of the window. I knew that I had no choice but to do this now. Whether I liked it or not Amelia and Alyssa were right. It was time to face this. I couldn't run away from the past any longer.

I thought that this trip was going to be easy and peaceful. Little did I know I was wrong. This year would be the one that changed my life forever. For dark secrets would be revealed.

―――

Chapter 2

Reliving The Past

Our plane finally landed in Pensacola. As I walked off of the plane Caleb grabbed my arm. "Don't worry. You can do this." Caleb told me. "There's nothing to be afraid of." Amelia said as her and the others stood behind us. "I know. I'm just getting the courage up I guess." I told them. We walked out of the airport and loaded up into a couple of cars that Darren had bought for our arrival. We drove off toward the city to go to my mother's house to visit her grave.

As we drove around in the city I looked out of the window and saw that we were down town. We were on Palafox street. As we kept driving I saw a girl sitting outside of one of the bars. She was sitting on the side walk and looked as if she was about to pass out. "Stop. Go park over there in the parking lot." I told Mason. "Why?" Mason asked. "Just do it." I replied.

I got out of the car and saw Darren pulling up beside us. "What are you doing?" Darren asked. "I'll be back in a minute." I told him. "I'm coming with you." Alyssa said as she got out of the car. I walked across the street toward the bar where the girl was sitting on the side walk. As I got closer I noticed that it was Ashley. I grabbed Alyssa by the arm and pulled her toward me.

"What is it?" Alyssa asked. "It's Ashley." I replied. "What?' Alyssa said in disbelief. Mason and Caleb walked up behind us to see what was going on. "What are you two doing?" Caleb asked. "That's Ashley. She was my roommate at the college." I replied. "What?" Mason said.

"She looks terrible. I've got to go and see if she's ok." I said. "Elizabeth, Ashley came to the house when the sheriff told mom that you were dead. You can't just pop out on her like this. You will scare her to death. Literally." Alyssa said.

"Ashley was my best friend babe. I agree with Elizabeth. We need to check on her." Mason said. "This is not like Ashley to be at a bar or to even be drinking." Mason added. "Something must really be wrong." Alyssa said. "What's going on?" Darren asked as he walked up behind   us with the others.

"Elizabeth just spotted a girl that use to be her friend." Caleb said. "I can't just stand here and watch her like this. Ashley looks like she needs a friend and she was a friend to me when I needed one." I told them.

"Alright." Caleb said. "Mason you stay here with me. It's going to be hard enough for Ashley to see Elizabeth." Alyssa said. "We need to give Ashley one heart attack at a time." Alyssa teased. "Alright." Mason agreed with a laugh. I walked over toward the bar where Ashley was. She looked rough. Ashley had on grey sweats and her hair was sticking out in all different directions. She looked like she had been through hell.

Alyssa stood back with the others observing while I made my way toward Ashley. I walked up toward Ashley slowly so that I wouldn't scare her. I thought that she probably wouldn't recognize me since I could smell the alcohol on her breath. Once again I was wrong. "Ashley?" I said.

Ashley looked up at me then stood up slowly. She looked like she was drunk as a skunk. She was clinging on to the wall for support so she could stand up. I could see the mascara that was running down her face. Ashley looked as if she had been crying for hours.

To be honest Ashley looked like crap to be a prep. Ashley moved. a little closer as she kept her hand on the wall. I could see the fog that was coming out of her mouth as she breathed. It was winter time.

One of my favorite times of the year. "Elizabeth?" Ashley said as she looked at me confused and scared to death. "Yes." I replied. Ashley jumped back looking scared to death like a little child. She looked just like Alyssa the night we had crossed paths.

"Your dead! How can you be here?" Ashley said as she was going into a freak out mode. "It's difficult to explain." I said in a calm voice. Ashley began to look at me with fear in her eyes and face a full of fright. "A demon! You're not real!" Ashley yelled as she started running out toward the road.

"Ashley!" I screamed as I ran after her. "Elizabeth!" Alyssa yelled. Before I could make it all the way across the road to the other side a car came out of no where and hit Ashley. Her body flew up and hit the windshield of the car and then she rolled off of the hood and hit the ground. The car came to a stop as I ran to Ashley's side. Mason followed behind me along with the others.

"Ashley!" I yelled. I rolled Ashley over toward me and held her body in my arms. Luckily she was still breathing. I could smell her blood as it ran down the side of her face. I called out to Caleb in order to keep me distracted from the smell. The blood was so sweet that I was tempted to feed on her. I fought the urge and the hunger with every ounce of strength I had in me.

"Caleb!" I yelled. "Well here we go again." Darren said as he ran over with the others. "Caleb, go inside the bar and tell someone to call an ambulance." I told him. "Alright." Caleb replied. "Alyssa, Ashley's leg has a nasty gash in it. Find me something to tie it off with." I told her.

"Ok. Come on Mason." Alyssa said. As Alyssa and Mason ran off I checked to see if Ashley was still breathing. The driver got out of the car and began to panic. " Oh my god! I'm so sorry!" The woman continued to stand by her car while I held Ashley in my arms.

"Is she still breathing?" Darren asked. "Yeah. Ashley's unconscious but she's still breathing." I replied. As I held Ashley 's body in my arms as I waited for the ambulance to arrive I looked across the street to see a woman and a boy who looked to be my age staring back at me.

The woman seemed to look at me as if she knew me while the boy seemed to look at me with curious eyes. I guess that was because I was a vampire and my friend was a human.

I looked back down to check on Ashley. After a moment I looked back up and saw that the woman and the boy were gone. It was as if they had vanished. Something inside me was telling me that something was wrong.

I knew that something was coming but I couldn't place my finger on what it was. Life as I knew it was about to become even more unbearable. Alyssa came back with a couple of rags and broke my train of thought.

"Here you go." Alyssa said. "Thanks." Caleb came out of the bar shortly after Alyssa handed me the rags. "The ambulance should be here in a few minutes." Caleb said. I nodded as I put the rags on

Ashley's leg in order to tie off the wound so that she wouldn't lose anymore blood than she already had.

Darren stood beside me along with Caleb to make sure that I didn't lose control with the scent of Ashley's blood in the air. "How is she?" Mason asked. "From what I can tell she's ok. She's still breathing which is a good sign." I replied. I kept holding Ashley in my arms as we waited for the ambulance to arrive.

"Amelia? Do you know them?" I asked. "No, I've never seen them before." Amelia replied. "Maybe their new to the city." Star said. "Maybe but the woman looked at me as if she knew me." I replied.

"What did they look like?" Caleb asked. "The woman had dark brown hair with golden highlights. It was long and curly like mine but her eyes were different. Her eyes like a golden topaz color with a hint of bronze. She was very beautiful. She was a little taller than me and was almost as smell as Amelia." I replied.

"And the boy?" Darren asked. "The boy had long hair to his shoulders. It was jet black. His eyes were the same as the woman's." I replied. Caleb looked at me and then glanced over at his brothers. They all looked as if they knew something I didn't.

Just before I could ask what was going on the ambulance had finally arrived. Caleb and the others stepped out of the way so that the paramedics could bring the stretcher out of the ambulance. One of the medics came over with a bag while the other two paramedics brought over the stretcher. As the man started going through his bag he began to ask me some questions.

"What happened here?" The man asked. "My friend went to cross the street and a car came out of nowhere and hit her." I replied. The medic looked over at the woman who was standing by her car. "Are you the owner of this vehicle?" The medic asked. "Yes. I'm so sorry I didn't even see the girl." The woman replied.

"My friend has been unconscious since the accident and she has a nasty gash in her leg. I tied the wound off to keep her from losing more blood." I said. "Ok. We will take it from here." The medic replied.

I put Ashley's body on the ground gently and stood back with the others so that the paramedics could get Ashley up into the ambulance. One of the paramedics came back over and asked me more questions. "What is your friends name?"

"Ashley Phillips." I replied. "Alright." The paramedics said. "What hospital are you taking my friend to?" I asked. "West Florida." I nodded as the man turned around to get into the ambulance. As the ambulance drove away I stood there wondering if Ashley would remember what had happened. Naturally Amelia beat me to the punch. "She probably will." Amelia said.

"Can't you stay out of my head for two seconds?" I asked. "No. I had way too much fun annoying you." Amelia replied as she put her arm around me. "I guess I'll just have to endure it." I said in a sarcastic voice. "That's right my girl." Amelia replied. I turned around to speak to the others. "I'm going to follow the ambulance to the hospital so I can check on Ashley." I told them.

"Are you sure that you should do that? I mean what if Ashley wakes up and she remembers everything and starts screaming?" Caleb asked. "Don't worry I can handle it. It will be alright." I replied. "Well here we go again." Victor said smiling. "Alright. You can go but we are going to follow you in case you get into a jam." Caleb said.

We walked back over toward the parking lot and got into our cars. When we got to the hospital we stood out in the front beside the sliding glass doors so that we could come up with a game plan.

"Amelia, can you sense Ashley?" I asked. "Yes. She's on the third floor." Amelia replied. "Which window?" Mason asked. "The third one on the right." Amelia replied. "I'm going to go around the back and come at the window from the side so that I won't be seen." I told them.

"Caleb and I will go into the hospital and meet you in the room." Amelia said. "What about the rest of us?" Darren asked. "You can come with us while the others keep a look out." Caleb said. I ran around to the side of the building and looked for the window. It was open. Easy access, I thought.

I could hear the wind as it blew in through the window. I leaped up to the window and climbed in. Ashley was laying in the bed sleeping. I walked toward the bed to get a closer look at her.

Ashley had a cut on the side of her eyebrow along with a few bruises on her cheek. There was still a little blood in her beautiful blonde hair. I could smell the blood off of her clothes that were sitting in a bag on the chair that was next to the bed.

As I stood next to the bed staring at Ashley I had all kind of guilty feelings that were running through my mind. Once again it seemed as if I had put another person in danger. Only this time it wasn't just any person. It was my best friend. I knew that Darren and the others were getting close.

I could smell them. I sat down in the chair beside the bed and reached out to take Ashley's hand. I began to speak to Ashley even though I knew that she wouldn't be able to hear what I was saying.

"Ashley, I want you to know that I'm sorry. I'm so sorry for all of this. I never should have approached you. If I had kept my distance you wouldn't be in here now. I guess I let my human emotions get in the way." I told her. "If a vampire has any human emotions." I teased.

"Your going to come out of this   and be ok. I believe that. I just want you to know that you will always be my best friend and I will always be with you in spirit. The truth is I'm no longer like you. I don't belong in your world anymore. So I guess that this is goodbye my friend. I love you."

I felt a tear run down my face as I spoke those last words. I wiped the tear away quickly as I smelled Darren and the others coming closer. After a minute Darren and the others were standing in the doorway.

"I see Ashley's doing ok." Darren said. "Yeah." I replied. Darren came over and put his hand on my shoulder as he proceeded to speak. "There's nothing that you could have done Elizabeth."

"This isn't your fault." Amelia said. "Maybe not but if I hadn't approached Ashley she wouldn't be in this hospital right now." I replied. "Don't be so hard on yourself." Caleb said. "We better get out of here before Ashley wakes up." Amelia said.

"You guys go ahead. I'll be down in a few minutes." I told them. As the others leaped out of the window I could hear them as they landed on the ground one by one.

I knelt down to kiss Ashley on her forehead. As I turned around to walk toward the window I heard a voice. "Elizabeth?" I said as I walked slowly toward her. Ashley looked at me the same way that Alyssa had a year ago when we had crossed paths.

"How are you alive?" Ashley asked. "It's difficult to explain." I replied. "All this time I thought that you were dead and you were alive." Ashley said as she looked at me with face full of confusion. I knew that I had to come up with a good lie and a good one fast.

"I ran away." I lied. "What? Why?" Ashley looked as if she was heart broken from my words. "I don't know. I guess I just wanted to seek a new thrill." I lied again. "How could you leave me behind?"

Ashley asked in a hurt voice. "I never meant to leave you Ashley but it just happened."

I didn't like lying to Ashley but I would rather lie and have her hate me than tell her the truth and put her in danger. "What happened to me?" Ashley asked. "Don't you remember?" I asked. "No. I mean I remember a little bit but not much." Ashley replied. "Well what do you remember?" I asked.

"I remember being at the bar and drinking. Then I went outside and then I saw you." Amelia was right. Ashley was definitely going to remember seeing me. "Anything else?" I asked. "No. It all comes to a blur after that." Ashley replied. "You were crossing the street and a car hit you." I told her.

"A car?" Ashley asked in a disbelief. "I got hit by a freaking car!" Ashley said in shock. "Yep." I replied. "Damn, just my luck!" Ashley said in an irritated voice. "Don't worry. You will be out of here in no time."

"It's so miserable being in a hospital. " Ashley said. "How come your parents aren't here?" I asked trying to change the subject. "Their out of town. They went on a vacation." Ashley replied.

"They're in Tennesee exploring mountains." Ashley explained. "Where's Justin?" I asked. "We broke up. I caught him kissing another girl. That's why I was at the bar in the first place." I was completely speechless. I couldn't believe that Justin would do that to Ashley.

It was obvious that I had missed a lot and that there was a lot more going on than I knew. "Have you seen Mason?" Ashley asked. Once again I was forced to lie. I had to protect all of us as well our secret. "No. I haven't seen him since before I left." I lied.

"Well that sucks. I miss him so much. He was my best friend." Ashley replied. "What about the rest of the crew?" Ashley asked. "Crew?" I said as I looked at Ashley confused. "Yeah. You know, Jason, Paul, Shelly, and Deanna." Ashley replied.

"What happened to them?" Ashley asked. "I have no idea." I lied again. I started to talk about Justin again to change the subject. "So when did you catch Justin cheating?" I asked. "Yesterday."

"Damn. You two seemed so perfect for each other." I said in amazement. "Yeah. We were together for about six years." Hearing those words really threw me for a loop. "Elizabeth, it is clear to me that after six years of what I thought was true love and happiness that it turns out that the whole time I have been so stupid. My life means nothing." Ashley added.

"Trust me Ashley, your life means more than mine does." I told her. "Why do you say that?" Ashley asked. "Let's just say that ever since I left Pensacola my life has been pretty rough." I really wanted to tell Ashley the truth but I knew that I couldn't. She would freak out all over again.

I placed my hand on Ashley's head and leaned down to kiss her forehead. "Jesus Elizabeth!" Ashley said in panic. "What?" I said as I raised my head up. "You're freezing!" I looked at her and smiled.

"Of course I am silly. Its winter. Its cold outside." Ashley looked at me and stuck her tongue out. I just laughed at her.

"I've got to go but I'll come back and see you tomorrow night." I said as I turned around to walk out of the room. "Why can't you come during the day?" Ashley asked. I stood there thinking of another lie to tell her. "I have some things to do." I lied. "I will be here tomorrow night. I promise." I assured her.

"Alright." Ashley replied. I turned back around and opened the door as I walked out of the room. As I walked down the hall I kept my head down hoping that no one would recognize me. Everyone seemed to stare as if they knew me but as usual they would turn away and go back to doing their job.

I took the elevator to get to the first floor. It didn't take me long to get outside where Caleb and the others were waiting for me. As I came outside I saw the others standing out in the front door. "So how did it go?" Mason asked.

"Well Ashley's awake." I replied. "She knows who I am and she asked me about you." I added. "What did you tell her?" Mason asked. "I told her that I haven't seen you since the day that I disappeared. I told her I ran away." I replied.

"Did Ashley believed you?" Alyssa asked. "Yes." I replied. "I don't think we have anything to worry about." I assured them. "We better get going. The sun will be up in about an hour." Darren said. "Ashley made me promise her that I would come back and see her tomorrow." I told them.

"I don't know if it's a good idea." Caleb said. "I'm going to come back and see her. I promised her and I won't break my promise. Ashley has already a broken heart as it is." I said. "Broken heart?" Mason asked. "Yeah. Justin cheated on her. That's why she was at the bar." I explained. "That jerk! I'll break him in half!" Mason said in an angry voice.

"Calm down." Alyssa said as she put her hand on Mason's shoulder. We started walking back toward the parking lot where the cars were. As we drove back home I sat in the back seat looking out the window. I wondered if our house looked the same or if some kids had found it and spray painted it or busted it up. When we arrived at the house I noticed that it still looked the same.

The house was still in the same condition that it was when we left. The house was still made of stone and was still standing. The lights were still burning outside around the porch. As I made my way up the steps I felt Caleb's hand on my arm pulling me back. "Are you really going to tell Ashley the truth?" Caleb asked.

As Caleb looked at me I could see the worry in his eyes just as I could hear the panic in his voice when he asked me that question. "No." I lied. "There's no need to lie Elizabeth." Amelia said as she walked by. "I won't be upset if you tell Ashley the truth. I'm just worried." Caleb said.

"I wish Amelia would stay out of my head. I would like to be able to think or speak without her interference." I said in an irritated voice. I turned around and looked out into the beauty of the night time sky as I crossed my arms over my chest. "Amelia is just worried about you." Caleb explained. "Amelia means no harm." Caleb informed me as he put his hand on my shoulder. "I know."

"I didn't mean to snap. I just feel like I owe it to Ashley to tell her the truth." I explained. "I mean she was my best friend before I became a vampire." Caleb looked down for a moment with a sad look on his face. He looked as if my words had stabbed him through the heart.

"Elizabeth if I could back to that night and change what I did I would." Caleb said as he stood there looking into my eyes. "No. You would have done the same thing. You would of done it because you love me too much to lose me. You would rather keep me here in eternity than let me go in mortal death." I replied.

"You kept me in the shadows with your immortal kiss. What's done is done and we can't go back but we can go forward." I added. Caleb looked at me as if my words had an effect on him. "Your right. If I could do it all over again I would have done the same thing. My love for you is beyond eternity. Its everlasting. You're like a drug that I can't live without and just like an addict I have to have you or I'll go crazy." Caleb said with a light smile.

"I love you Caleb Macbeth." I said as I pressed my lips to his and put my arms around his neck. "I love you too." Caleb replied. "I know that you don't agree with my decision but I know that Ashley will keep our secret." I told him.

"Well if you trust Ashley I can trust her." Caleb said as he took me into his arms. "You should sleep. You have a long night ahead of you." Caleb added. I took Caleb's hand into mine as we walked into the house. As I walked down the stairs to the cellar where the others were I could hear them arguing about Ashley.

"I think Elizabeth knows what she is doing and I think that Ashley is a nice girl." Amelia said. "I agree." Star replied. "What if Ashley screws up and tells someone?" Victor asked. "She won't." Mason said.

"Ashley's not like other humans. She's a good kid and she doesn't deceive others." Mason added. "Well here we go again." Darren said. "Looks like we have another Alyssa in our hands." Darren teased as he looked over at Alyssa and smiled.

"I think it would be nice to have Ashley in the family." Alyssa said. "I second that." Amelia said. As I stepped down from the stair case and began walking toward the others Amelia looked as if she knew what I was getting ready to say.

"Ashley is my best friend and just because I'm a vampire now does not mean that I'm going to ignore her. I feel that I owe it to her to be honest. I have already hurt Ashley enough as it is. She deserves better from me." I explained.

"Elizabeth." Victor said. "I understand your concerns Victor but even you would have to admit that in the past I have done nothing but tried to protect this family." I said interrupting me. "I have also put my life on the line for this family as well." I added. Everyone stood there in silence as Victor walked toward me.

"Yes you have but my deepest concern is for the safety of this family. You of all people should be able to understand that." Victor replied. "I understand your point Victor but you must see mine. I would never betray this family and neither would Ashley." As the others continued to stay silent Victor began to speak again. "Alright. I can see that everyone else here trusts you and so do I even though I'm out voted."

"Thank you Victor. I know that this can't be easy for you but your support means a lot to me." I said as I leaned forward to hug him. As I walked over toward my bed I thought of how I was going to tell Ashley the truth. As I laid down on the bed and closed my eyes I had a flash back of when I told Alyssa the truth. Then I had the flash back of when I took Alyssa's soul.

My mind was made up and under no circumstances I was going to take Ashley's soul. I would not let her become one of us. My plan was simple. I was going to enter Ashley's room tomorrow night and tell her the truth that she deserved to hear. Then I was going to disappear once again with my family. Somehow that seemed easier said than done.

nice again my dreams came to haunt my subconscious. I dreamed that Ashley and I were running through a field of beautiful flowers but the strange thing about it was that it was sunny. I was in the sunlight chasing after her and playing along the field and I did not burn.

I wished more than anything that it wasn't a dream and that it was real. I wished that I could feel the warmth of the sun again. In the moment of that I thought I began to see the light fade away and dark clouds roll in over us. The weather became dark and stormy as the night made its way in.

As I stood there looking confused I could see Ashley as she kept running through the field toward the woods. It was as if she didn't notice the change of the weather at all. I called out to Ashley many times but she kept running.

I began to run after her only to end up in the dark woods. As I entered the woods I saw Jade holding Ashley by the throat. As I screamed Ashley's name I could hear the sound of Jade's hands breaking all of the bones in Ashley's neck.

After that tragic moment Jade started to run off. I wanted to follow her but as I tried to run I couldn't. My feet stayed on the ground and I couldn't move. Once again I was confused. It was in that moment that I saw my mother appear in a bright beautiful glowing light. She was in a white dress and looked as if she was an angel from the heavens.

As I called out to my mother she remained silent. I began to get even more confused. That was when she lifted her hand to point at a woman and a boy. It was the same woman and boy that I had seen in the street when Ashley got hit by that car.

That was when mother spoke and told me to go to them. I turned back around to look at my mother as she began to fade away into the sky. That was the moment I woke up.

As I turned my head to look over at Caleb he was awake. He was laying beside me staring into my eyes. He was staring at me with worry. We were the only ones in the room. The others had already woken up and went up to the living room.

Once again I had slept the day away and night had come again. "Are you alright?" Caleb asked. I laid there for a moment not sure of what to say. "I'm fine." I lied. I was actually quite puzzled but I was more confused than anything. "You don't seem fine." Caleb said as he began to worry.

"I just had a weird dream." I replied. "What about?" Caleb asked. "It was about Ashley. I saw mom and then I saw those two vampires from last night and then I saw Jade."

Caleb sat up as if he had seen a ghost when I mentioned the two vampires from the night of Ashley's accident. "Why do you look at me weird every time I mention the vampires I saw?" I asked.

"If I tell you then will you tell me about your dream?" Caleb asked. "Yes." I replied. "Tell me about your dream first." Caleb said. "I was running through a field with Ashley. It was sunny." Caleb smiled as if he was recalling his days in the sunlight when he was a human. "Then the sun faded out and the clouds began to roll in and it was dark."

"That doesn't sound good." Caleb said. "It wasn't. Ashley kept running as I called her name. I ran after her and ended up in the woods. It was like a big dark gruesome looking forest.

When I got into the woods I saw Jade holding Ashley by the throat as she cracked every bone in Ashley's body. I tried to move toward them but I couldn't. It was like there was some magnetic force that was holding me to the ground." I took a deep breath and continued.

"Then out of no where mom appeared in this big, bright, glowing ball of light. She had a white dress and looked like an angel. The next thing I know is mom is pointing out toward the two vampires I saw in the street last night. Mom said something that was really weird."

"What did she say?" Caleb asked looking as if he knew something. "She told me to go to them. It was really weird." Caleb sat there for a moment of silence. He looked as if he was thinking hard about something. I spoke again to break the silence. "So are you going to answer my question?" I asked. "Yes but promise me that you won't be angry with me." Caleb replied.

"Why would I be angry with you?" I asked looking confused. "Just promise." Caleb said once more. "Ok. I promise." I replied. "Alright. The reason I look at you weird when you mention those two particular vampires is because I know them." I looked at Caleb with a confused look again. "How much do you know them?" I asked.

"The woman is Mary Collins and the boy is her son Shane Collins." Caleb said. "So why would I be angry with you for knowing them?" I asked confused once more. "Mary Collins was from Pensacola just like you and Alyssa are. Mary was human when she met a vampire named Bradley Collins. Mary conceived a son before Bradley turned her. Shane. Shane is a hybrid. He is half human and half vampire but that's another story. Before Mary met Bradley and became a vampire she was married to a human named Will Meadows. They had a child together."

"So what's the point?" I asked. "One night Will was killed by a mugger leaving Mary a widow. A month after Will was killed Mary gave birth. It was a girl. Mary put the child on a family's door step. After that night no one in Pensacola ever saw her again. The humans anyway. Its been almost eighteen years since my family and I saw Mary until now." Caleb replied. "So how do you know her?" I asked.

"I met Bradley after he turned Mary. Bradley had came into town to visit me and brought Mary and Shane along so I could meet them. Shane was just a baby that time. Anyways, Mary told me that she had a human daughter and that she wanted me to keep an eye on her daughter and that she wanted me to keep an eye on her daughter while her and Bradley were away in Germany raising Shane. So I did as Mary asked and I watched her daughter as she grew and I looked for her."

"What happened to the girl?" I asked. "She got caught up in a bad situation." Caleb replied. "Is what why Mary and her son are back?" I asked worried. "Yes. Its more than that though." Caleb replied. "This is the part where I told you not to be angry with me." Caleb added. That was when his beautiful emerald eyes looked into mine. Suddenly I had a nervous feeling inside.

I wasn't sure how I knew it then but I knew that the next words out of Caleb's mouth would be hard for me to hear. "The reason why Mary is here is because her daughter is alice." Caleb said. "She is not human though. Mary has come back to see her child as well as to take revenge upon me for turning her child into a vampire." Caleb explained.

"So you have turned someone before?" I asked. "Yes." Caleb replied. "Ok, so when Mary comes after you we will be prepared. We will fight with every means we have." Caleb started shaking his head. After a moment he spoke again. "I don't think your going to want to fight Mary." I sat there looking at Caleb confused once again. Why would he say that? This wasn't making any sense at all.

"Why?" I asked. "This is going to be hard for you to hear but Mary is more than just a vampire." Caleb replied. "What is she?" I asked.

"Mary is your mother." I felt the confussion fade away. Anger began to fill up in my face now. I couldn't believe what I was hearing. "That's not funny Caleb!" I said in an angry voice as I got up off of the bed.

"I know its not." Caleb said in a soft voice. "She is not my mother! My mother is dead!" I yelled. "How could you say this to me?" After a moment I turned around and started walking up the stairs. That was when Caleb grabbed me by my arm. "Elizabeth, please don't be angry with me." Caleb said as he held my arm. "Angry? I'm not angry. I'm furious!" I said in a harsh tone.

"What would even make you think that I was Mary's child? I asked as I snatched my arm away from Caleb's grip. "Because Mary led me to you the night that her and Bradley came into town. The night that she asked me to look out for her child." Caleb replied.

"So Mary led you to me?" I asked in disbelief. "Yes. I have been watching you ever since that night. You weren't even a year old." Caleb replied. "My family and I had to leave every few years or so in order to keep the humans from getting suspicious about us since we never age but I always managed to come back and keep an eye on you." Caleb explained.

"Does Darren and Victor know about this?" I asked. "Yes. My brothers and I are the only ones who know. Amelia and Star have no idea." Caleb replied. "I can't believe you right now!" I said as I turned around to walk up the stairs again. Caleb called after me.

"Elizabeth! Elizabeth, please come back!" Caleb yelled. I stopped walking and turned around to face him. "I'm going to the hospital to visit Ashley and I'm going to tell her the truth. When I'm done there I'm going to find Jade and kill her so that she won't be able to hurt Ashley or anyone else for that matter. When all of this is finished I'm going to find Mary and find out exactly what she wants." I turned back around and walked up the stairs and out of the room.

When I walked into the living room I saw everyone standing there looking at me as if they knew what had just happened. Of course with Amelia in the house who wouldn't know. I opened my mouth and began to speak as I walked toward the door. "I don't want to talk about it." Amelia stepped out in front of the others and walked over toward me.

"Elizabeth, we didn't know until now." Amelia said. "Darren and Victor knew." I replied. Amelia turned around to look over at Darren. "Is that true?" Amelia asked. "Yes." Darren replied.

"Caleb made us swear that we wouldn't tell anyone." Victor said. "Elizabeth, I know your angry. You have every right to be but please don't leave Caleb because of this. He was just trying to protect your heart. He knew that you would never believe him. He didn't want to hurt you." Darren said.

"After your mother died Caleb could see how much pain you were in and he didn't want to cause you more pain by telling you the truth." Victor said. "How could you two keep this a secret from us?" Star asked. "I guess you two couldn't confide in your own wives." Amelia said. "I know you and Victor were just trying to honor Caleb's wishes but he still should have told me the truth." I said.

"I'm sorry Elizabeth." Darren said. "Its alright. Its just sad that I can't even depend on my own husband to tell me the truth. My whole life has been nothing but a life." I replied. Amelia just stood there looking as if she was about to explode with anger. She was just as furious with Darren as Star was with Victor.

"Caleb told me about Mary and Will. He also told me about Bradley and Shane." I told them. "Well at least he told you." Victor said. "There's just one thing that I don't understand. Why did Mary give me up?" It couldn't have just been because Will got killed." I said looking confused.

"It wasn't." Caleb said as he entered the room. "I think that we should all leave the room and let Caleb and Elizabeth talk." Stair said. As the others left the room I walked over toward Caleb. "Then what was the reason?" I asked.

I stood there with my arms crossed over my chest once again waiting for Caleb to respond. After a moment he did. "Do you remember when Astarte told you that you would find out everything in time?" Caleb asked. "Yes." I replied.

"Mary didn't want to give you up but she had no choice. Elizabeth, you have always been meant for more than you thought. A few months after Mary gave you up she was living on the streets. She was in so much pain after your father was killed that she prayed for death." Caleb explained.

"One night Bradley was walking down Olive Road. He saw Mary passed out on the side of the road. She was drunk on Vodka. Bradley fell in love with her as he looked into her soul.

It was in that moment that Bradley decided to take Mary back with him to a little town called Jay. It was there in Jay at Bradley's home that he nursed Mary back to health. Bradley also helped Mary with her depression and her drinking problem." Caleb added.

"So what happened next?" I asked. "After a month Mary was clean and her and Bradley conceived Shane." Caleb replied. "So that's why Shane is a hybrid?" I asked trying to understand everything. "Yes. He's half human and half vampire. Shane is the only hybrid to our knowledge." I still couldn't believe what I was hearing. It was very hard to process all of this hidden truth.

"So your telling that I am Mary's child and that she is here to take revenge upon you for turning me?" I asked. "Yes." Caleb replied. I still couldn't believe all of this. "So does Alyssa know that her mother adopted me?" I asked. "She does now. This is new to her as well. Alyssa is just shocked as you are about all of this. Amelia filled her in" Caleb informed me. "Oh great." I said in a sarcastic voice. "How much more complicated could things possibly get?" I asked in a sarcastic voice once again.

"I'm sorry Elizabeth. I know your mad at me and you have every reason to be." Caleb said. "I was just trying to do what Mary had asked of me as well as protecting you from more pain." Caleb explained. "I just need time to figure all of this out." I replied. "Of course.' Caleb said as he put his arms around me. I still couldn't believe all of this. This was just too much to handle.

I couldn't believe that everything that I had ever known had been a lie. I felt as if I had been living one big lie my entire life. "We should get to the hospital." Caleb said. "We?" I asked looking confused. "Yes. You may need me there if Ashley gets out of sorts when you tell her the truth." Caleb replied.

"After all I am a good voice of reason." Caleb said with a slight smile. I was still mad at Caleb but I knew that he had a point. I decided to let him go with me. "Yeah. I guess you are. Let's go." I told him.

We made our way out the door and headed toward the hospital. I didn't know how I was going to tell Ashley the truth but I knew that she deserved to hear it. Ashley was my best friend. I knew that if the situation were reversed that she wouldn't lie to me. This was something that I had to do no matter what the consequences were. I owed it to Ashley.

Chapter 3

Breaking The Ice

I stood there below the window to Ashley's room wondering how in the hell I was going to explain all of this to her. That was when Caleb began to speak in order to give me a piece of mind. "Just tell Ashley the truth." Caleb said. ""How did you know what I was thinking?" I asked looking confused. "I can read souls." Caleb reminded me. "Yes but not minds."

"True but it doesn't take a mind reader to know what your standing here thinking about. The look on your face is obvious." Caleb replied. I turned back around to look up at the window where Ashley's room was. I was getting ready to leap up toward the window when Caleb put his hand on my arm.

"What is it?" I asked. Caleb had his eyes closed as if he was trying to focus hard on something. "Its Jade. She's near." I began to feel the fear of my dream coming true. "How close is she?" I asked. "Very close. She's back in the woods watching us."

"I've got to get to Ashley." I replied. "Alright. I'll stay down here and keep Jade from getting in." I leaped up toward the window and made my way into Ashley's room. As I came in through the window I saw Ashley laying in the bed sleeping. Luckily she didn't see me come in. I put my hand on Ashley's arm to wake her.

"Ashley?" I said in a soft voice. "Ashley wake up. Ash?" I called out. "Elizabeth?" Ashley said as she opened her eyes. "Yes." I replied. "What are you doing here?" Ashley asked. "I came back to visit. Remember?" Ashley looked at me confused for a moment but then she looked as if she remembered something. "Oh yeah. I'm sorry I forgot. I've been having trouble remembering things lately." Ashley replied.

"That's ok. I've got to get you out of here. Caleb is waiting outside for us." I told her. "Who's Caleb?" Ashley asked. "My husband." Ashley looked at me in shock. "Your husband? Oh my god! You got married?" Ashley asked as she stared at me in disbelief. "Yes but that's another story. You have to get out of here now." Ashley kept looking at me with a confused look.

"Why?" Ashley asked. "No time to explain. We have to hurry." I said as I pulled her out of the bed. "Elizabeth wait! I---." I picked Ashley up off of the bed and put her on my back. "Put your arms around my neck and hold tight!" I yelled as I ran toward the window. 'Wait! Elizabeth! What the--?" In that moment I had jumped out of the window. As I waited to make my landing I could hear Ashley screaming.

"Oh my god! We're gonna die! Elizabeth!" Ashley yelled. I just rolled my eyes as I finally landed on my feet. Ashley's arms were still wrapped around my neck. I stood there waiting for her to let go. She was still hanging on my back. Caleb couldn't help but to laugh. I turned my head slightly to speak to Ashley.

"You can let go now." Ashley opened her eyes. As soon as she felt the ground she hopped down and slowly released her grip from around my neck. Ashley stood back to the side looking at me like she wanted to kill me. "Are you out of your freaking mind!" Ashley yelled. "Ashley calm down." I said.

"I'm going to find a car." Caleb said. "Oh great. Leave me with the crazy human." I said in a sarcastic voice. "Yeah good luck with that." Caleb teased.

Ashley stood there looking confused. "How much in the hell did you that? Ashley asked. "I'll explain later. Right now I need to get you to safety. I'm taking you to my house and then I'll explain everything." I replied.

"No you explain now!" Ashley yelled. In that moment Caleb pulled up in front of the hospital with a car. It was black Pontiac. "Get in the car." I said as I turned to look at Ashley. "No! Not until you explain!" Ashley yelled. "Get in the damn car!" I yelled back.

Ashley moved toward the car quickly and got in the back seat. I walked around the car and got in the passenger seat. As Caleb drove us back toward the house I sat there thinking about Jade and how far behind us she was now.

Jade was always a fast tracker. She was almost as fast as Vladimir and just as good. That was a scary thought in my mind. Especially the dream I had about Ashley. We finally made it to the house after a thirty minute drive. As we pulled up in front of the house Ashley started to ask questions again.

"Are you going to tell me what's going on?" Ashley asked. I got out of the car and walked around to open Ashley's door so she could get out. "Yes but first I need to get you inside." I replied. I grabbed Ashley's arm and walked toward the house while Caleb walked ahead of us to open the door.

As I walked through the door with Caleb the others began to stare at Ashley. They were smiling and keeping their distance as I walked with Ashley over toward the couch. As Ashley sat own on the couch I turned toward the others to introduce her. "Everyone this is my friend Ashley."

Everyone greeted her with a smile. "Alyssa?" Ashley said as she stood up slowly. "Is that really you?" Ashley asked. "Yes." Alyssa replied. "Oh my god!" Ashley said in an excited voice as she went over to hug Alyssa. Mason stepped out in front of Darren throwing Ashley for a loop.

"Mason?" Ashley said in disbelief. "Hey Ash." Mason said. Ashley walked over to hug him. After a moment she flinched back. "Your so cold." Ashley said as she stood back running her hands down her arms.

"Yeah we get that a lot." I said. "Caleb?" I called. "Yes?" Caleb said as he walked up toward me. "Fill in the others about Jade while I speak to Ashley alone." I replied. "Of course." As the others left the room I began to speak to Ashley.

"What's going on?" Ashley asked. "Ashley, everything that you know is about to change. You are about to cross over into a world that you don't understand. One that you would have never imagined." I explained. "Elizabeth, what are you talking about?" Ashley asked. I went over to sit down on the couch. "I never ran away." I replied. "So what really happened?" Ashley asked as she came over to sit down beside me.

I got caught up in the middle of a robbery and I was shot. Caleb found me and changed me. Caleb found me and changed me." Ashley sat there staring at me in disbelief. "Changed you?" Ashley asked confused. "Yes. I'm a vampire."

Ashley sat there in silence for a moment. Finally she began to speak. "A vampire?" Ashley said in disbelief. "Yes." I replied. Ashley sat there on the couch in silence once again. She looked as if she didn't know what to say. Finally she started to laugh. "Your going to have to do better than that." Ashley said laughing.

I sat there for a moment thinking of how I could prove to Ashley that I was a vampire. Finally the thought came to me. I looked at the room. I turned to look at Ashley with a smile on my face as I began to walk up the wall.

When I got to the ceiling I stood there as I hung upside down and watched the expression on Ashley's face. After a moment I flashed down next to Ashley and sat on the couch next to her.

Ashley looked up at me with a face full of fear and jumped up off of the couch and kept my distance. I knew that I had frightened Ashley enough already. Ashley stood back against the wall looking as if she was terrified. She was completely frozen in fear. "Its alright. I know your afraid. This is a lot to take in at one time." I told her. Ashley remained silent.

I spoke again in the hopes that I would calm her down. "I'm not going to hurt you. Now you understand why I couldn't show myself after what happened. Now you know why I had to stay hidden. I didn't want this but it was chosen for me. Please don't hate me. I understand if you don't want to be my friend anymore. I just wanted you to know the truth."

Ashley opened her mouth and began to speak. "I don't hate you. I'm just having a hard time trying to understand all of this." Ashley said as she got up off the couch and walked toward the center of the room. I got up off the couch and walked toward her.

I stopped a few feet away so that I wouldn't make her feel uncomfortable. "I know that this is hard for you but now that you know what we are I have to ask something for you." I said. "What?" Ashley asked. "Please do not tell anyone about us. You must keep our secret." I told her.

"I won't tell anyone. I promise." Ashley assured me. "Thank you." I replied. "So all of this time you haven't been dead?" Ashley asked. "No. Well I am dead but not in the way you thought I was." Ashley looked at me confused once again.

"So is Alyssa a vampire too?" Ashley asked. "Yes. I turned her last year." I replied. "So would you turn me?" Ashley asked as she walked toward me. "Absolutely not!" I said outraged as I stated to walk out of the room. "Why the hell not?" Ashley asked in a harsh voice. "You did it to Alyssa!"

"Alyssa was different!" I yelled. "How?" Ashley asked as she crossed her arms and looked at me with a mad face. "She was dying!" I yelled once again. "What?" Ashley said in disbelief.

"It's a long story." One that you shouldn't be concerned with." I replied. "So all of you are vampires?" Ashley asked. "Yes. Including Mason." I replied. "How did he become a vampire?" Ashley asked. "The same way Alyssa did. They were both dying when they were changed. I changed Alyssa and Caleb changed Mason." I explained. "So are Shelly and the others vampires too?" Ashley asked.

"No. They were all killed by Vladimir." I replied. "So why are you so against changing me?" Ashley asked pressing the issue once more.

" I mean I'm your best friend." Ashley added. "Exactly." I said in a soft voice. "You don't want this believe me." I added.

"Isn't that my choice?" Ashley asked. "You don't know what your asking. Being a vampire is not like you think it is. Trust me." I walked across the room toward the window. As I looked out of the window I started to speak again. " I live everyday regretting what I am. I also have to live with the fact that I am responsible for taking Alyssa's soul." Ashley came over to stand beside me.

———

"What you do you mean your responsible for taking Alyssa's soul?" Ashley asked. "Once you're a vampire you have no soul. Its like your soul is in limbo. Like its kind of in between worlds." I explained. Ashley looked at me as if she felt sorry for me. "Treasure your humanity for as long as you can. You may not see it but humanity is precious. I would give anything to have my humanity back." I added.

"So why did you take me out of the hospital?" Ashley asked changing the subject. "I had a dream that you were killed by a vampire." I replied. "Why would a vampire be after me?" Ashley asked worried. "Her name is Jade. She is after me for killing her maker." I replied.

"Why did you kill Jade's maker?" Ashley asked confused. "Because her maker killed my mother." Ashley looked at me in surprise. "Your mom is dead?" Ashley asked in shock. "Yes. She's been dead for a year now. That's why I came back here. I wanted to pay my respects." Ashley put her hand on my shoulder. "I'm sorry to hear that. Your mother was a good woman."

"Yeah. Well right now the main focus is keeping you safe from Jade." I replied. "Oh great. So I'm at the top of the food chain now. Wonderful." Ashley said in a sarcastic voice. I couldn't help but to laugh at that one. "Pretty much." I replied. "So what do we do now?" Ashley asked. "I'm going to find Jade and lure her away from you. In the mean time you can stay in the guest room upstairs."

"What about the other vampires?" Ashley asked worried. "My family won't harm you. Amelia tends to dig around in other people's minds though. When they least expect it." I replied. "Oh. For a moment there I thought you were going to tell me that Amelia was going to eat me." Ashley said looking relieved. "No. Amelia is one of the sweetest creatures of our kind. She's very loving." As soon as I finished that sentence Amelia walked into the room.

"I hear someone talking about me." Amelia said as she reached out to put her arm around me. "Yes. I was telling Ashley how sweet you are." I replied. "Oh Elizabeth, your so sweet. If I was still human I would feel all warm and fuzzy inside." Amelia said as she smiled at me.

I smiled back at Amelia as I hear Darren laugh as he came into the room with the others. "My wife has just much humor as I do." Darren said as he looked over at Ashley. "I'm starting to see that." Ashley replied. "So what's our plan?" Caleb asked. "You and I are going on another hunting spree." I replied.

"You and I will track Jade and keep her as far away from Ashley as possible while the others stay here and protect her." I added. "Got it." Caleb replied. "Star and I will guard the house from the outside." Victor said.

"Well Amelia, it looks like we got the baby sitting job again." Darren teased. "Your just so good at it." I said as I pinched Darren's cheek. "So we're all in agreement then?" I asked as I looked around at everyone. "Yes." Mason said as he and Alyssa entered the room.

I started to follow Caleb toward the door when Alyssa reached out to grab my arm. "What about me and Mason?" Alyssa asked. "You two can help Victor and Star guard the house." I replied. "Alright." Alyssa said.

"Damn! I wanted to go on the hunt." Mason said. "I know but Ashley needs all of the protection that she can get while Caleb and I track Jade." I said. Mason nodded in agreement as I turned around and walked toward the door.

As I placed my hand on the door knob Ashley began to speak. "Elizabeth? Are you sure that I'm safe with all of these vampires?" Ashley asked worried. "I mean it's a little scary knowing that your in a house with a bunch of vampires that want to eat you and stuff." Ashley added. Darren naturally couldn't help but to laugh. I cracked a smile along with Caleb as I turned around to speak.

"You will be fine. I promise. Trust me." I said as I put my hand on Ashley's shoulder. "Ok but if I die I'm going to be really mad and then I'm going to come back and haunt you." Ashley said as she shook her finger at me. "Bye Ashley." I said as I turned around and walked out the door.

As I stepped out into the night with Caleb I could feel the cool breeze of the night blow pass me. "Let's get started." I told Caleb. We started to fly through the night to begin our hunt for Jade. I was prepared for the hunt and to find Jade and kill her. I just wasn't prepared to find a certain vampire in the woods waiting for me.

Chapter 4

The Return Of Old Friends

Caleb and I had been on the hunt for Jade for what felt like hours. It was in that particular moment when I caught a smell of death. Once that I would have thought was Jade's but as I moved closer I could tell that it wasn't hers. It was a smell of another vampire. A smell that I hadn't been around in a year. In that moment I heard a voice behind me.

"Hello Elizabeth." The voice said. I recognized the voice immediately. I turned around quickly. "Bell?" I said. "Yes." Bell replied as she moved the hood of her black cape away from her face. "Oh Bell!" I said in an excited voice as I walked over and hugged her. "Oh Bell! I've missed you so much." I said as I wrapped my arms around her neck. "So have I my dear."

"What are you doing here?" I asked. "I'm tracking Jade. Her scent led me here." Bell replied. "What are you two doing out here?" Bell asked. "We're tracking Jade as well." Caleb replied.

"Jade is after my friend Ashley." I said. "Who's Ashley?" Bell asked. "It's a long story." I replied. "Its so good to see you." Caleb said as he went over to hug Bell. "Where's Benjamin?" I asked.

"Is someone talking about me?" Benjamin asked as he stepped out from behind a tree. Benjamin was standing there in his dark blue jeans and grey hooded jacket with a smile on his face.

"Benjamin! Its so good to see you." I said as I went over to hug him. Benjamin lifted me up into his arms and spun me around. "Its good to see you too Elizabeth." Benjamin said as he put me back down on the ground. "Hello Benjamin." Caleb said.

"Hello Caleb." Benjamin replied. "So did I just hear you telling my wife that you two are out here tracking Jade?" Benjamin asked. "Yes." Caleb replied. "I had a dream that Jade was after my friend Ashley." I said.

"Who's that?" Benjamin asked. "Long story." Caleb replied. "Well Benjamin and I will do all that we can to help." Bell said. "Raven is going to leave Sky with Pandora and Astarte and then she's going to head this way." Bell added. "Sky and Serenity have become quite the play mates." Benjamin said. "I bet." Caleb replied.

"I had a vision that Jade was here. Raven is going to help me track her." Bell said. "I'm surprised that you didn't see Ashley in the vision." I said. "Yeah me too. I saw enough though. Ever since then Benjamin and I have been out tracking." Bell replied.

"I take it that you haven't found Jade yet." Caleb said. "No." Benjamin replied. "What all did you dream about?" Bell asked. "I dreamed that Jade killed Ashley and then I dreamed about two vampires. One woman and a young boy." I replied.

"What?" Bell said as she looked as if she knew something. "Yeah. I saw them the night that Ashley got hit by a car. We were waiting for the ambulance to come when I saw them from across the street. They were looking at me as if they knew me." I replied. "Oh boy." Benjamin said.

"What?" I asked worried. "Did you tell Elizabeth about those two vampires?" Benjamin asked. "Yes but she doesn't believe me." Caleb replied. "Well you better start believing Elizabeth. Mary and Shane are here because of you." Bell said. "So everyone keeps reminding me." I said as I looked at Caleb.

"If everything goes right Raven's plane should land tomorrow night." Benjamin said. "Good. We could use all of the help that we can get." I replied. "We need to find Jade first so that your friend will be safe and then we need to find Mary and find out what she wants." Benjamin said.

"She wants Elizabeth." Caleb replied. "She also wants revenge on me for turning Elizabeth." Caleb added. "I'm not so sure." Bell said. "Why do you say that?" I asked. "Its just a feeling." Bell replied. "We need to get going. We have a lot of ground to cover." Benjamin said.

I followed Bell and Benjamin as Caleb followed behind me. We decided to split up in order to cover more ground. We stayed close by in case one of us ran into Jade. We searched the words until an hour before sunrise. As we started heading back home I knew the others would be happy to see Bell and Benjamin again.

As we walked back home I kept thinking about Mary. I was just as curious as the others talk about why she was here but most of all I couldn't believe that my whole life had been based on nothing more than a lie. That was the worst part of it all.

I guess their right when they say that the fairy tale goes on for so long and then eventually you have to grow up and leave it behind. Everyone was pleased to see Bell and Benjamin when we got home. Especially Amelia.

Amelia and Bell were like Alyssa and I. They were like peanut butter and jelly. As we walked into the living room everyone was lounging around. Amelia ran up toward us as soon as she saw Bell enter the room.

"Bell!" Amelia yelled as she ran over to give Bell a hug. "Oh my goodness. Its so good to see you." Amelia said as she was bursting with excitement. "You as well Amelia." Bell replied. "What brings you two here?" Amelia asked.

"I had a vision that Jade was in the area." Bell replied. "I'm going to kill her if it's the last thing I do." Bell added. "Well think its time for all of us to turn in." Victor said. "Yeah. I'm quite tired." Bell replied. "Where's Ashley?" I asked. "She's upstairs sleeping." Darren replied.

We all headed straight to bed and woke up the next night to meet in the living room where we talked about our plans to find Jade and Mary. I sat on the couch next to Alyssa and listened to Bell speak to the others about how we were going to find Mary. Ashley was still upstairs sleeping. She was really exhausted.

"Raven is going to arrive soon. I think we're going to need more help though. As a matter of fact I think that we're going to need the help of the Brotherhood again along with the help of some others." Bell said.

"Why is that?" Victor asked. "We're not only dealing with Jade. We're also dealing with Mary and where Mary's concerned so is Shane as well as Bradley." Benjamin replied. "We need to find Jade and kill her before she has the chance to get to Ashley." Bell said as she looked over toward me.

"I don't understand why Jade would be after your human friend. It just doesn't make any since. Its not her style." Caleb said. "I can't think of any other reason why Jade is after Ashley other than to make me suffer for killing Vladimir." I replied.

"You've got a point." Caleb said. "We haven't seen them since early 1900's. It will be good to see them again." Amelia said. "We need to call the airline and arrange a flight to Alaska. We need to get the siblings here as soon as possible. I fear it is not safe here in Pensacola anymore. Not for Ashley anyway." Bell said.

"What do you mean?" Ashley asked as she came down the stairs. "She means that we're going to Alaska and taking you with us."

Benjamin replied. "What?" Ashley said looking worried. "Ashley this is Bell and her husband Benjamin. Their vampires from Italy." I told her.

"Its nice to meet you Ashley." Bell said. "You too." Ashley replied as she shook Bell's hand. "What if the Alaskan vampires try to eat me? Then what?" Ashley asked looking worried. "They won't" Darren said laughing. "Their just as nice as Astarte and his family." Caleb assured Ashley. "Who's Astarte?" Ashley asked. "He's the father of all vampires." Amelia replied.

"First we wait for Raven to arrive and then we go to Alaska and talk to siblings. Then we go to Ireland and enlist the help of the Brotherhood." Bell said. "Agreed." I said. "Who's Raven and who's the Brotherhood?" Ashley asked. "Raven is a friend of ours." Star replied. "The Brotherhood is Astarte and his family. Their the oldest vampires on earth." Alyssa said.

"In the mean time we just need to sit here and wait until Raven arrives as well as protect Ashley." Bell said. "Elizabeth, you need to go down town to Palafox Street and see if you can find Mary." Bell added. "Why do I need to find her?" I asked. "You need to find out what it is that she wants." Bell explained. I nodded in agreement. "Come on Caleb. Your going with me." I said.

———

Caleb and I went into the city in hope that we would find Mary. We walked down the side of Palafox Street. I could see the humans hanging around in front of the bars. They were drinking and stumbling all over the place. It kind of reminded me of when Caleb and I would walk down the streets in the French quarters of New Orleans.

We came around to the bar where Ashley had been. I looked around for a moment and caught the scent of a vampire after a few minutes. That's when I saw Mary. She was standing over in an alley by one of the bars. I nudged Caleb's arm as I looked over at her.

"What is it?" Caleb asked. "Look." After a moment Caleb looked over and saw Mary. Caleb and I began to walk over to the other side of the street where Mary was standing. She stood there in the alley eyeing us intently.

I started to speak as Caleb and I entered the alley. "Hello Mary." I said. Mary looked at me like she hadn't seen me in years. "I know you're mad at me for turning Elizabeth but I had no choice. She would have died if I hadn't turned her." Caleb said.

Mary looked at Caleb as she began to speak. "I'm not upset with you Caleb. I understand. I'm not after you. I just wanted to see my child." I looked at Mary with a furious expression.

"I'm not your child!" I snapped. "Elizabeth." Caleb said as he grabbed my arm. "NO! I had a mother and she died. Vladimir killed her." I said as I jerked my arm away from Caleb's grip.

In that moment Mary looked as if she was heart broken. "Vladimir killed that woman that took her in?" Mary asked as she looked over at Caleb. "Yes he did." Caleb replied.

Mary looked back over me with such sadness in her eyes. "I'm very sorry Elizabeth. I'm sure that Lisa was a very good mother to you when I couldn't be." Mary said. "She was the only mother that I had and she was great." I replied. "You are not my mother." I added in a harsh tone of voice.

"So why are you here Mary?" Caleb asked. "Julian is after me. I need your help." Mary replied. "What? Julian! Are you serious?" Caleb said in a frustrated voice. "Who is that?" I asked. "Julian and his two siblings Melina and Estard run things over in that area." Caleb replied. "While Julian ids the king of Egypt his siblings are the prince and princess of that country." Mary said. "Oh Great." I said in a sarcastic voice.

"Alright Mary, what did you steal?" Caleb asked as if he already knew she had done. "It's a poison that Julian had his witch Olivia made. It's very powerful." Mary replied. "What does it do?" I asked. "The potions can allow a vampire to walk into the sunlight. Forever." Mary replied. "You mean that is really possible?" I asked in a hopeful voice.

"Yes. The potion gives you the power to walk into the sunlight forever like the pureblooded vampires can." Mary replied. "Why did you steal it?" Caleb asked. "Because I wanted to be able to walk into the sunlight. I'm so tired of these dark nights. I'm willing to give the potion back though. Julian has something that I want."

"What does Julian have?" I asked. "My husband. Bradley." Mary replied. "Julian has Bradley?" Caleb asked "Yes. Julian captured Bradley during my attempt to steal the potion. He's keeping Bradley as a hostage until I bring him the potion." Caleb looked as if he was irritated as he started shaking his head. "Damn Mary! I can't believe that you would mess with Julian. He's even worse that Vladimir was." Caleb said in an irritated voice.

"That's why I need your help. Help me save my husband and in return I will do something for you." Mary Pleaded. "Like what?" Caleb asked. "I know that you desire to walk into the sunlight

Caleb, You miss it more every day." Caleb looked as if Mary's words had an effect on him. "How does she know that?" I asked looking confused. "Mary can read emotions of a vampire." Caleb replied. "Alright Mary, I'll help you." Caleb agreed.

"Thank you." Mary replied. "Have you drank any of the potion?" Caleb asked. "No. I'm waiting until I get Bradley back so he and I can drink it together." Mary replied. "Well if you and Bradley drink the potion then how could you give it to me?" Caleb asked confused.

"Julian has a whole case full of the stuff. There's enough for you and your family as well as your friends if you all choose to drink it." Mary replied. "We have another situation as well." I said butting in.

"We have to go to Alaska as well as Ireland." I said. "You're going to see Astarte?" Mary asked. "Yes." Caleb replied. "How do you know Astarte?" I asked looking curious. "Every vampire knows Astarte. He likes to keep in touch with every being of his kind for we are all his children." Mary replied.

"Caleb and I will take you back home with us. We will go to Alaska to enlist the help of the siblings and then we will go to Ireland to see Astarte. Once we have done that we will go with you to Egypt." I said. "Agreed." Mary replied. "Raven should be arriving soon." Caleb said.

"Where's Shane?" Caleb asked. "He's out in the woods hunting.

I'll have to go get him." Mary replied. "Elizabeth and I will come with you." Caleb said. "That would be great. Elizabeth should meet her brother." Mary replied in an excited voice.

"He's not my brother!" I said in a harsh tone of voice. "Elizabeth, be nice." Caleb said as he put his hand on my shoulder. "We would be glad to come with you Mary." Caleb added. "Follow me."

Caleb and I followed Mary out of the alley and back into the city. We began to make our way put toward the woods. I didn't like any of this but for some reason I just went along with it. Part of me seemed rather excited to meet Shane but the other part seemed to dreading it. Whether I liked it or not I was getting ready to meet my brother. Half brother. All I could do was just make my way through this like I did everything else.

Chapter 5

Shane

As Caleb and I followed Mary through the woods I could hear the cracking sound of bones breaking but they weren't human bones. In that moment I caught the smell of a coyote. Not too long after I caught its scent the scent of its blood followed. "Shane is nearby." I said. "Yes. He's feeding on an animal." Mary replied. As we walked out into the woods I saw him. Shane. He was drinking the blood of the coyote he had caught. I stood there next to Caleb in the clearing wondering what was going to happen next.

"Shane!" Mary yelled. He turned around to look at her. When Shane's eyes met with mine he dropped the coyote on the ground. "This is Elizabeth and Caleb. They are here to help us." Mary added.

Shane moved toward us slowly. He stopped a few feet away as he looked over toward me. I could see the blood in his face. That was strange to see considering that he was a vampire but then I remembered that he was a hybrid. He was half human.

"So you two are going to help my mother?" Shane asked. "Yes. I replied. Shane looked at me with a curios look on his face. It was the same look that he had given me the night Ashley had her accident. "So you're my sister?" Shane asked.

"I am absolutely nothing to you or your mother. I'm only here to help." I replied. "Why are you so bitter?" Shane asked, "I have my reasons." I replied in a cold voice. "Fair enough." Shane replied with a slight smile on his face. "So I guess we should head to Egypt and visit our dear friend Julian." Shane said in a sarcastic voice.

"We have to go back with Caleb and Elizabeth to their home first. They have a situation that they have to deal with." Mary said. "What could be more important?" Shane asked. "I have a friend that needs my help." I said. "Would that be human friend that I saw you with the other night?" Shane asked with a slight smile on his face.

"Yes." I replied. "Well in that case I think my mother and I will go with you. I would love to get to know your friend." Shane said with a big smile on his face once again.

"If you touch my friend I swear that I will make you wish that you never had." I said in threatening voice. "Well aren't you just a little ball of sunshine. I guess you really are my sister." Shane teased. "Go to---." Caleb moved forward to put his hand over my mouth.

"Let's just get to the house." Caleb said cutting me off. We began walking to the woods toward the house as Shane and Mary followed behind us. When we got to the house I saw Star and Victor standing outside on the porch. Victor was grinning from ear to ear.

"I see that you found what you were looking for." Victor said as he looked at me with a slight grin on his face. "Yes we did." Caleb replied. "Elizabeth, Bell had another vision. She needs to talk to you immediately." Star said.

"Alright." I replied. "Who are they?" Shane asked. "Their part of Caleb's family." Mary replied. "Has Raven arrived?" I asked. "Yes. She just made it in." Star replied. "Let's Get inside." Caleb said.

As we walked into the house everyone was standing in the living room as if they had been waiting for our arrival. Everyone looked over toward Shane and Mary as they entered the room.

"Well I see you brought back your friends." Darren teased. I looked over at Darren with an angry face. "Ok. Shutting up now." Darren replied as he crossed his arms. I looked across the room to see Raven standing by Amelia.

I walked over across the room to hug Raven. "Hello Raven." I said as I wrapped my arms around her neck. "Hello Elizabeth." Raven replied. I turned back around Raven's neck. "We have another problem." I told them. "What kind of problem?" Benjamin asked. "A big problem. " Caleb replied. "Mary stole a potion from Julian." Caleb added.

"Julian?" Darren said looking worried. "Yes. The potion that Mary took from Julian is one that allows a vampire to be able to walk into the sunlight forever. Like a pureblood can." I replied. "You mean that's actually possible?" Amelia asked in a hopeful voice.

"Yes it is." Mary replied. "Why did you steal the potion Mary?" Raven asked. "I wanted to be able to walk into the sunlight again. I wanted to feel as human as I possibly could. I miss my humanity." Mary replied.

"Don't we all." I said as I crossed my arms. "So what is the potion made of?" I asked. "Julian's blood." Shane replied. "Other than Shane and Astarte Julian and his family are the only day walkers of our kind. They are the only purebloods that we know of to exist." Mary said.

"Vladimir was the only other pureblood besides Astarte along with Julian and his siblings." Shane said. "The only reason why

Shane can walk into the sunlight is because he is a half human." Mary said.

"I see." Amelia said. "We have to go to Egypt and give the potion back to Julian in order to get Bradley back." Mary said. "Julian has Bradley?" Darren asked. "Yes. This is what I meant by a big problem." I replied.

"We have to go to Alaska and get the help of the Alaskan siblings so that they can help us track down Jade." Bell said. "That's right. We have to protect Ashley." Alyssa said. "We have to find Jade and kill her." Benjamin said. "As you can see we have a lot on the agenda." I said as I looked over at Mary.

"I can see that." Mary replied. "Alright, here's what we will do. We will go to Alaska first and talk to the siblings to see if they will help us. Then we will go to Ireland and enlist the help of Astarte and his family. Once we have everyone together then and only then will we go to Egypt." I told them.

"Is everyone in agreement?" I asked. "Yes." Victor replied. "We are all behind you Elizabeth." Amelia said. "I agree." Raven said. "Mary? Shane? Are you in?" Caleb asked. Shane looked over at Mary and nodded. "We're in." Mary replied.

"Then let's get ready to go to Alaska." I told them. "I'll call the airline and arrange our flight." Caleb said. "I'll take Ashley upstairs and get her some clothes. As small as she is she should fit into my gear." Amelia said.

"Elizabeth, you don't have to do all of this for me. I'm not worth all of this trouble." Ashley said. "Yes, you are." Shane said as he looked over Ashley and smiled. "Ashley you are my friend and friends protect each other. I will fight forever if I have to in order to keep you safe." I told her.

"Well going Alaska and Ireland could be kind of cool." Ashley replied. "Going to Egypt would be cool if only I wasn't going to die there." Ashley added. "You are not going to die! I won't allow it! Don't think like that." I replied. "Ok, ok, calm down." Ashley said as she put her hand on my shoulder.

"Come on Ashley. Let's get you upstairs to change." Amelia said. While Ashley went upstairs with Amelia I sat downstairs with the others waiting. "I like your friend." Shane said. "I think when all of this is over I just may turn her." Shane added. "Over my dead body!" I yelled as I stood up ready to lunge at him.

"That's enough!" Mary yelled. "How can you turn a human anyway?" I asked. "You're half human." I added. "That's one of the great things being a hybrid. Not only we are unique but we can turn humans as well. Of course, they're not born a vampire like we are but we can make them a vampire." Shane replied.

"How can you make someone a vampire when you're only half of one?" Star asked. "When we bite a human we can make them half vampire beings that we're born a hybrid." Shane replied. "So instead of becoming a vampire they become a hybrid?" Star asked. "Yes." Shane replied. "Any human that I turn will be half human and half vampire just like me." Shane added.

"That makes a lot of sense." I said in a sarcastic voice. "Doesn't it though?" Shane replied with a big smile on his face. I stood there in the living room waiting with everyone while Amelia was upstairs with Ashley.

Caleb finally came back from calling the airline. "Alright everything is set. Our flight leaves at nine so we need to hurry." Caleb said. "Mason and I will be outside by the cars waiting." Darren replied. "Alright." Alyssa said.

"Wait. We only have two cars. How are Bell and the others going to get there?" I asked. "We can fly there or we can just run through the forest." Raven replied. "I can run into the city real fast and get another car." Caleb said. "There's no need for that. I think we can fit everyone in both cars?" Star replied.

"How?" Victor asked. "Caleb and I will be in the first car with Alyssa and Mason. I can sit in Caleb's lap while Bell sits in Benjamin's lap." I replied. "Problem solved." Benjamin said with a big smile on his face as he put his arms around Bell.

"I guess since Darren and Amelia will be in the front of the second car then I can sit in Victor's lap and put Raven and Ashley beside us." Star said. "That's fine with me." Raven replied. "Then its solved then." Caleb said. "Shane and I will go through the woods and meet you at the airport." Mary replied. In that moment Amelia and Ashley came down stairs.

Everyone looked up at Ashley in amazement. She looked stunning in Amelia's dark blue jeans and silver sweater along with her grey boots. I guess Amelia made sure that she dressed warm since we were going to Alaska. The rest of us didn't have to worry about dressing warm beings that we were vampires. We stayed cold all the time. We were use to it. "Darren and Mason are waiting outside by the cars." I told them. "Who am I riding with?" Ashley asked.

"Your going to ride with Amelia. You don't have anything to worry about. Amelia will take good care of you." I replied. "Alright." Ashley agreed. "Alright everyone lets go." Caleb said. As we walked out of the door I began to wonder what was going to happen when we reached Alaska.

I wondered if the siblings were going to help us or not. I was hoping that we weren't making this trip for nothing. I knew that I could count on Astarte to help us but we really needed everyone that we could get to help us with our mission. This time everything was different. There seemed to be much more at stake this time than there was last time. Everything was different this time around.

Only one thing managed to be the same. This time I was fighting for everything and everyone that I cared about. I didn't want our trip to Alaska to be a total failure. I was hoping to enlist the help of the Alaskan siblings along with the Brotherhood.

I was prepared for whatever awaited us when we reached the Alaskan clan's territory. I was also prepared to fight for my family. However, I was even more prepared to fight for my best friend's life. Even if it meant losing my own.

Chapter 6

Alaska

As we got off the plane when we made it to Alaska I started to have the same feeling that I had when we came to Ireland to go before the Brotherhood. I felt that same nervous feeling that I had before. I wasn't so sure that I had made a good decision by coming into unfamiliar territory but I knew that if Bell had faith in them as well. This was something I had to do.

"So where do the Alaskan siblings live?" I asked. "They live in a huge two story house just beyond the mountains." Bell replied. "The siblings like their privacy." Benjamin said. "I just hope that they don't eat me." Ashley said. Darren started to laugh. "Their not going to eat you." Amelia replied.

"I wouldn't mind a taste." Raven teased. "See Elizabeth, I told that our friends want to eat me." Ashley said as she began to panic. Everyone started to laugh. "I'm not going to eat you. I was just teasing." Raven replied. "Oh. Well that makes me feel so much better." Ashley said in a sarcastic voice. As soon as we got outside of the airport we started heading toward the woods.

As we walked through the woods I started to get a strange feeling. I felt as if someone was watching me. I stopped waling and started looking around. After a moment I closed my eyes and began to listen to see if I could hear anything. "What is it?" Caleb asked as he walked up behind me.

"I feel like we're being watched. I think there's something out there watching us." I replied. "What is it Bell?" Raven asked. "It's Jade. She's here. She's out there watching us." Bell replied. "Where is she?" I asked. "How close is she?" Caleb asked.

"Very close. She's getting ready to attack." Bell replied. "Come out and face us Jade!" Bell yelled. In that moment I could hear foot steps coming out of the woods behind us. "Well, if it isn't the Italian psychic." Jade said. "Hello Jade." Bell replied.

"I see you brought the human with you. She will be a great snack after I kill all of you." Jade said in a cold voice. "That's not going to happen." I said as I stepped out in front of the others. Amelia and Raven stayed close to Ashley as Shane stepped out in front of them.

"Well hello Elizabeth. Its been a long time. The last time we met you killed someone that meant a lot to me." Jade said as she moved forward. "Its not like you haven't done the same thing." Bell replied in a harsh voice.

"Yes. Your human friend. I just want you to know that it was like music to my ears when she begged for her life before I ripped her throat out." Jade said with a smile on her face. Bell growled and ran toward Jade but Benjamin grabbed her by the arm and pulled her back.

'Why are you after Ashley?" I asked. "Because you killed my maker. You killed the one person that mattered to me the most. The only person that I have ever loved. So I think that its only fair that you lose your best friend before I take you out. I want you to experience what it feels like to lose something that you love." Jade replied. "Vladimir never loved you." Caleb said.

"Yeah. I guess I can see your point but there's just one problem." I said as I stepped in front of Caleb. "What's that?" Jade asked. "Your going to have to get through all of us before you can get to Ashley." I replied. "I wouldn't have it any other way."

Jade leaped toward me and knoced me back into a tree causing it to break in half and fall to the ground. I got up quickly and ran toward Jade once again while Bell and Star tried to hold her off from Ashley. Benjamin, Caleb, and Victor jumped in to help me bring Jade down. As Jade knocked all of them back on the ground I grabbed her by her hair and threw her across the clearing of the woods.

Raven, Mason, Mary and Darren stepped in to help me while Amelia, Alyssa, and Shane stood back in front of Ashley to protect her. "Amelia, keep Ashley back!" I yelled. Jade got up off of the ground and came at me again. I stepped out of her way and flashed over behind her.

As I tried to grab Jade from behind she flashed back behind me and kicked me back into the trees. Raven tried to grab Jade but she was too fast for her. Shane and Mary ran toward Jade and try to catch her but she knocked them back into the trees as well. As I got up from the ground once again I saw Jade turn and run through the woods. In just a matter of seconds she vanished. She was gone.

"Is everyone alright?" I asked as I stood back up on my feet. "Yeah. We're fine." Caleb replied. "I don't understand why she would run away if she was willing to take all of us on." Mary said. "She's waiting until Ashley's alone so that she won't have to fight all of us. We took her by surprise." Bell replied.

"Well Ashley won't be alone. We will make sure that she is protected at all times." Amelia said. "Agreed." Shane said as she looked over and smiled at Ashley. Ashley started to blush. "Lets get to the Alaskan siblings before Jade decides to come back." Alyssa said. "She won't come back until Ashley is alone." Bell replied. "Come on everyone. Lets get going." Caleb said.

We walked through the woods for about another hour before we reached the mountains. It was really beautiful. It kind of reminded me of the mountains in Tennesee. I could feel the snow on my skin as it fell. I could also feel the cool breeze that blew all around me.

If I was still human I would have been freezing in this kind of weather. It was so beautiful the way the snow covered the mountains. As I looked out pass the mountains I saw a huge two story house.

It was built out of wood. It had a walk way filled with lanterns. The lanterns were burning out in front of the house. The flames looked so warm. Too bad I couldn't feel heat anymore. Its strange what you miss when you no longer have it. "Alright, we have to get over the mountains in order to reach the house where the Alaskan clan is." Bell said. "How do we get over the mountains?" Ashley asked.

"We can jump over them and be there with in seconds but one of us is going to have to carry you on our back." Amelia replied. "Oh no! I hate heights. Forget it!" Ashley said as she stood back looking scared. "Its ok. All you have to do is put your arms around my neck and hold on tight. You can just close your eyes. It won't take long. It will only take a minute." I assured her.

"Ok. I can do this. After all I'm just a human. What could happen right?" Ashley said as she walked over toward me slowly. "Benjamin and I will go first and then the rest of you can follow."

Bell said. I stood back with the others while Bell and Benjamin jumped up on top of the mountains.

"Wow! Damn yall can jump high!" Ashley said in a shocked voice. "We can do a lot of things." Mason replied. "Come on babe. We're next." Alyssa said as she took Mason's hand. Raven, Amelia, and Star jumped next. Now it was my turn to go up with Ashley. Caleb stayed down with me in order to help keep Ashley calm.

"Are you alright?" Caleb asked as he put his hand on Ashley's shoulder. "Not really. I'm just scared. I think I may be getting sick." Ashley replied. "Its ok to be afraid." I replied. "That's easy for you to say. You're a vampire. Your not human like me." Ashley said as she put her arms around my neck.

"I may not be human but If I had the opportunity to be a human again I would do it in a heart beat." I replied. "Make sure you hold on tight." Caleb said. "Are you ready?" I asked. "No but I don't have a choice." Ashley replied. "Close your eyes. It will be over in a minute." I jumped up toward the mountains as Caleb followed behind me. It only took us a minute to reach the top.

"You can open your eyes now." I said as I landed on the ground.

Ashley opened her eyes and looked around. Once she saw that we were on top of the mountains she released her arms from around my neck. "Wow. I thought that was going to be scary but it wasn't." Ashley said in a surprised voice.

"I told you." Caleb replied. "Come on everyone." Bell said. I felt nervous once again as we began to approach the house where the Alaskan siblings were waiting. All I could do now was hope that they would be as gracious as Astarte was. As we walked toward the steps I could see the flames inside the lanterns as they danced around inside of the glass.

The flames seemed to shine as bright as the stars in the sky. "This is the place." Bell said. "Its now or never." Raven as she put her hand on Ashley's shoulder. Caleb walked up the steps and knocked on the door. A dark haired man with mint green eyes opened the door. He was a vampire just like us. I could tell by the way that he smelled. "May I help you?" The man asked.

"I am Caleb Macbeth. I am here with my family. We need to speak to the Alaskan siblings." Caleb replied. "Come in." The man said. As we walked inside the house I noticed that it was set up kind of like the house that we had in Pensacola. There were pictures on the walls as well as furniture scattered around in the room.

The house looked like a cozy and comfortable place. There was a fire place as well as candles lit all around. "This way." The man said. We started to follow the man down a hall. It was a long hall way with wooden walls and a grey marbled floor. As we walked down the hall I saw more pictures on the wall.

They didn't seem to look as old as I thought they would be. As we got to the end of the hall I saw a big room with four chairs made out of stone that were setting in the middle of the room. As I looked over I saw a fire place as well as more pictures and candles. What is it with vampires and pictures and candles?

As I looked back over the chairs I saw four people sitting in them. There were two girls and two boys. Each of them had blonde hair and blue eyes. Their eyes were like a midnight blue color. They were so beautiful. I guess they call them siblings because they all look the same.

"Everyone this is the Alaskan clan. Lex, Athena, Eve, and William." The man said. "Thank you Joseph. That will be all." Lex said. "Yes my lord." Joseph replied as he walked out of the room. "Hello Bell. Its good to see you again." Eve said. "You as well Eve."

Bell replied. "I see you have brought quite a few friends with you." Athena said.

"Yes. My friends and I need your help." Bell replied. "What's wrong?" Lex asked looking worried. "A lot of things." I said butting in. "My name is Elizabeth. This is my friend Ashley." The siblings looked as if they were amazed. "A human?" William said surprised. "Yes. This human is my friend." I replied.

"As you may have heard Vladimir is dead. I killed him. Because of that Jade is after my friend." I explained. "Julian is involved as well." Benjamin said. "Julian? Why on earth would he be involved?" Athena asked looking confused. "Mary, would you like to explain that one?" I asked as I looked over at her and smiled.

"Of course." Mary replied. "I stole a potion from Julian. Because of my foolish actions he is holding my husband Bradley hostage until I return what belongs to him." Mary explained. "What value did this potion have for you to act so foolishly?" Eve asked. "It is a potion that is made from Julian's blood. One sip from the potion and you can walk into the sunlight forever." Mary replied.

"So its true then? That is really possible?" William asked. "Yes." Shane replied. "Will you help us get Bradley back and stop Jade? Bell asked. Lex turned to look at the others as if he was conferring with them. They looked at him as if they were all in agreement. "Of course." William replied.

"Thank you." Mary said. "We will also be going to Ireland to enlist the help of the Brotherhood." Caleb said. "We're with you until the end." Athena replied. "We;; now that we're all in agreement we need to get going." Caleb said. "Jade followed as here and tried to attack us on our way up." Bell said.

"We will do all that we can to help." Lex replied. "You all can rest here tonight. We have guest rooms up stairs." Eve said. "Jade won't be stupid to attack you here." William said. "Not unless she wants to die." Eve said with a slight smile. "Thank you." Darren replied. "Joseph will show you all to your rooms." Athena said.

"We will make arrangements to fly out soon as the sun goes down." William said. "Joseph!" Lex yelled. "Yes?" Joseph said. "Please show our guests to their rooms." Lex said. "As you wish." Joseph replied. "Thank you for your hospitality." Caleb said.

Joseph stepped toward the door to hold it open for us. "This way." Joseph said. We followed Joseph back down the hall as he led us toward the stair case. As we walked up the stairs I saw more pictures on the walls.

Surprisingly there were no candles but their were lanterns on the walls. I guess they were meant to light our way. Joseph stopped and turned to face us. "There are five rooms in this hallway take your pick." Joseph said. We all started to walk down the hallway as we looked around to see what room we wanted. "Enjoy your stay." Joseph said as he walked back down the hall.

Caleb and I took the first room. Bell and Benjamin took the last. Everyone else stayed in the rooms between us. "So who do I room with?" Ashley asked. "You can room with me if you want." Raven replied.

Ashley begain to look a little nervous. "I won't bite. I promise." Raven said trying to put Ashley's mind at ease. "I might." Shane said with a light smile. I punched him in the arm. "Hey! I swear Elizabeth your so violent." Shane said as he started to rub his arm.

"Better her than me." Ashley said with a slight grin. "Ok Raven. If Elizabeth trusts you than so do I." Ashley replied. "Follow me." Raven said as she grabbed Ashley's hand. As Caleb and I went into our room everyone else headed to theirs.

I went over and sat down on the bed. Caleb came over and sat next to me after taking a glance round the room. "So I guess this is as good a time as any to finish our discussion from before." Caleb said. "I guess so. I've had time to cool down." I replied.

"Look, I'm sorry that I kept all of this from you. After your mother died I saw how much pain you were in and I couldn't bare to tell you about Mary while you were in such a state."

"I understand. All of this is just shocking and very over whelming. Its just a lot to try and take in at once." I replied. "I'm sorry that I blew up but I just don't understand how you couldn't find the time to tell me. I mean I was with you and your family for five years before mom died. That's what I don't get." I added.

"I understand. Your right, I should have told you." Caleb replied. "Then why didn't you?" I asked. "I thought that you were better off not knowing. Elizabeth, I never expected any of this to happen. When Mary came to me and asked me to watch over you I did it as a favor to her. I never thought that any of this would happen. At least not like this.

"I get it." I replied. "Do you forgive me?" Caleb asked. "I don't know. Its kind of hard. I never thought that you of all people would keep something like this from me. I mean you're my husband." I replied.

"If I can't confide in you and trust you than who can I trust?" I asked. "I guess you can't trust anyone if you can't trust me of all people." Caleb replied as he got up off of the bed. "I'm tired. I'm going to turn in." I said. "I'm going to see my brothers. I'll be back in a little while." As Caleb walked out of the room I rolled over and closed my eyes.

I knew that my words had hurt him but I couldn't help but to be honest. I felt betrayed. "If I just get some rest maybe I'll be able to have a piece of mind." I told myself. I drifted off to sleep while Caleb was in the next room with his brothers.

"Well if you had just told her the truth to begin with then you wouldn't be in the dog house." Amelia said. Darren and Victor started to laugh. "Your in a tight spot brother." Darren said. "Oh you two aren't in a great spot either." Star replied. "You two lied as well." Amelia said.

"We were only respecting Caleb's wishes." Victor replied. "That may be, but you still could have told me." Star said. "Yeah Darren, why didn't you tell me about any of this?" Amelia asked. "Its like Victor said, we were respecting Caleb's wishes." Darren replied.

"You know I thought that we didn't keep secrets from each other. I guess I was wrong." Amelia said. "When are you going to let this go?" Darren asked. "I don't know. It depends on how long I want to press the issue." Amelia replied as she looked Darren with furious eyes. "Enough said." Darren said as he looked away.

While Amelia and Darren argued Raven and Ashley were getting along a lot better than I expected. "There seems to be only one bed so you can have it. I'll be fine on the floor." Raven said. "Oh, well that's very nice of you but you don't have to sleep on the floor. There's plenty of room." Ashley replied.

"Are you sure? I mean aren't you worried about me eating you?" Raven teased. "No. This may sound strange but I actually kind of like you even though you are a vampire. You seem like you're a nice person even though your technically dead." Ashley said with a slight smile.

"Well thank you. I'll take that as a compliment." Raven replied with a slight grin. "So what is it like to be a vampire?" Ashley asked.

"Miserable. Its like one big earth bound torture. A tragedy among tragedies. Well actually, I think it's the biggest tragedy of all." Ashley looked as if she felt some remorse for Raven.

"That sounds sad. I guess that's why Elizabeth wouldn't turn me." Ashley said. "That's part of it." Raven replied. "What else is there?" Ashley asked. "Could you imagine taking someone's life from them? Taking their soul?" Raven asked. "No, I can't." Ashley replied.

"Well that's what happens when you become one of us. Your soul is taken away and all that's left is just a body with a taste for blood that you can't even imagine." Raven explained.

"I see what you mean." Ashley said. After an hour Caleb finally got things straightened out between his family and walked back to the room. I was laying in the bed asleep. Once again I had a strange dream. I was running through the woods with Caleb laughing and playing around.

The strange thing however was that it wasn't night. It was day. We were running through the woods in the sunlight. After running for a while we came to a field that was full of flowers. There were all different kinds.

The field was full of gardenias, roses, babies breath, tulips, and sunflowers. It was a wide assortment of flowers. There was a river on the other side of the field that had a water fall. The waters were not black as night. They were blue. The water sparkled as the sunlight reflected off of it.

Everything seemed to be going perfect until I heard a cry coming from behind me. It sounded like a child. When I turned around I saw a baby laying on the ground in a basket. It wasn't a human child though. It smelled like a vampire. It was a beautiful baby boy.

He had a curly black hair and green eyes. I couldn't understand how that could happen beings that vampires can't conceive children. Then again, with Astarte being the first vampire to ever walk the earth I guess anything is possible.

In the moment of that thought everything seemed to get even stranger. The baby disappeared. I felt something jerk inside of my stomach. I put my hand on my stomach and felt something move. Suddenly I felt a kick and with that large sums of pain. I began to scream as I fell to the ground.

Before I could call out Caleb's name he was there beside me. I could feel whatever was in me trying to come out. It was worse than the agonizing pain I had felt when I was being turned into a vampire. I had never felt anything like this before. Finally I woke up and saw Caleb sitting on the bed beside me.

"What is it?" Caleb asked. "I had another strange dream." I replied. It was not like any dream I have ever had before." I added. "Do you want to tell me about it?" Caleb asked. "I dreamed that you and I were running through a field in the sunlight and then suddenly I heard a baby crying." Caleb looked at me confused. "A baby?" Caleb asked.

"Yes. It wasn't a human child. It was a vampire child." I explained. "That's weird." Caleb said as he looked completely surprised. "The next thing I know the child disappears and then I feel something moving inside of me. Then I started to feel huge amounts of agonizing pain." Caleb looked at me as if he knew something. "I'm sorry I was so mad at you before. It was all just very surprising."

"Its ok. I should have told you." Caleb replied. I reached out to put my arms around Caleb's neck as I leaned forward to kiss him on his soft lips. "I'm sorry I was such a pain." I said as I put my head on his chest. "As long as I have you I don't care about anything else." Caleb replied as he put his arm around me.

"You should get some sleep. You look exhausted." I said as I ran my fingers through Caleb's hair. "I will later. Right now I just want to hold you." Caleb replied. "Is that all you want to do?" I asked with a slight grin. Caleb looked at me as if he knew where I was going with this.

"Well now that you mention it, I think other ideas have come to mind." Caleb replied as he leaned forward to kiss me with a big smile on his face. It wasn't long before we were wrapped in each others embrace giving sweet comfort to another once again. As we slept the rest of the night away I had another dream. It was one that I never expected to have.

However, I do have strange dreams. I guess Caleb is right. I have the gift of seeing the future through dreams. This dream however seemed to be the strangest of all. I couldn't be certain of where I was but from the looks of everything around me it looked as if I was in Egypt. I was in a huge room that had a lot of Egyptian artifacts. As I turned around I saw Ashley laying on the floor in the center of the room.

I could hear her heart beat fading out. I could also see and smell the blood that was on her shirt. She was dying. I started to walk toward her but then I stopped as I saw Raven kneeling down beside her. Before I could say anything Raven began to feed on Ashley. I stood there looking confused. I didn't know what to say.

After a moment Ashley stood up and looked completely different. She was one of us. A vampire. I wanted to say something to her but before I could say anything I heard a door open. I looked over at the door and saw no one. All I could see was the sunlight as it glowed from outside of the door. When I looked back over toward Ashley she was gone.

I was getting ready to call out her name when I heard someone laughing. It sounded as if it was coming from outside the door. As I walked toward the door I saw Ashley running outside in the sunlight along with Shane through the same field of flowers that I had seen before. I started to smile at Ashley as she twirled around in the sunlight.

After a moment Ashley waved her hand for me to come out and join her. I walked out slowly. I felt no pain as I stepped out into the sunlight. I started laughing as Ashley took my hand as we started twirling around in the field. Everything seemed so wonderful until I looked down at Ashley's stomach.

She looked as if she was carrying a child. She looked like she was nine months pregnant. Ashley smiled at me as she noticed that I was staring at her stomach. She started to smile as she reached out to touch mine.

I didn't know why she was touching me at first but as I looked down I saw that my stomach looked the same as hers. Ashley turned and walked away with Shane as I stood there looking confused. I couldn't understand any of this.

None of this made any sense. It was in that moment that I woke up. As I sat up on the bed I saw Caleb looking up at me. "Are you alright?" Caleb asked. "Yeah. These dreams are just so weird." I replied. "Did you see the magic baby again?" Caleb teased.

"No. I saw Ashley becoming one of us." Caleb looked at me with a big smile. "Yeah. I could have told you that was going to happen." Caleb replied. "There's something else." I said as I looked at Caleb with worried eyes. "What is it?" Caleb asked.

"Ashley was dancing in the sunlight with Shane. She was carrying a child. She was pregnant." Caleb started to laugh. "Ashley and Shane get together?" Caleb asked. "Apparently so." I replied. "I can't wait to see that." Caleb said as he leaned over to kiss me on the cheek as he got up out of the bed.

"I was pregnant too. In the dream." I said as I sat up on the bed. "Really?" Caleb said as he looked away as if he knew something.

"Yeah." I replied. Caleb started to walk toward the door. "Where are you going?" I asked. "To see my brothers." Caleb replied.

"You need to get ready. We'll be flying out to see Astarte in a few hours." Caleb added. "Alright." I got up off the bed and went to sit in front of the mirror to brush my hair as Caleb walked out of the room. None of this made any sense to me. I knew that vampires couldn't have children.

The only way that Ashley could have a child with Shane was if she conceived a child with him before she became a vampire unless hybrids can conceive with each other. I decided to go and talk to Bell. She would know what was going to happen before any of us would. That's what I loved about her. Bell was like an open book. Like a book full of prophecies.

As I made my way to Bell and Benjamin's room I passed by Darren and Amelia's room. I could hear Star, Victor, and Caleb talking. I could hear Caleb talking to them about something that seemed to be bothering him. "It can't be possible." Caleb said. "It obviously is. Elizabeth is the one who killed Vladimir." Victor replied.

"Vampires can't have children unless its with a human." Darren said. "Not according to the prophecy." Victor replied. "All the prophecy said was that a human would kill Vladimir but as it turns out Zane was wrong because Elizabeth killed Vladimir not Alyssa." Amelia said.

"Yes, but Zane also spoke of a prophecy that said something about a vampire that was able to conceive children." Victor replied. "So you think its possible?" Caleb asked.

"It has to be. Why else would she of had that dream?" Victor replied. "What if we're wrong? Star asked. "What do you mean?" Darren asked. "Well Caleb said that Elizabeth had a dream that Ashley would carry Shane's child and become one of us." Star replied.

Now it was clear to me what they were all talking about. Apparently the dream that I had was a glimpse of the future. Ashley's future. "That could still happen. Amelia said. I started to walk on down the hall toward Bell and Benjamin's room. I knew that they were talking about the dream that I had about Ashley.

"It would be nice to have a son." Caleb said. "You should feel lucky brother. If this does happen you will have a child of your own." Darren replied. "Yeah. I guess I'm just worried over nothing." Caleb said.

I hurried along to Bell's room so that I could talk to her. I had to figure all of this out. When I got to Bell's room I saw her sitting in a chair by the fire place while Benjamin stood behind her. "Bell?" I said.

Bell turned to look at me as if she knew why I had came. "You heard Caleb and the others talking didn't you?" Bell asked. "Yes." I replied. "I'll leave so you two can talk." Benjamin said. "I haven't irritated Caleb in a while." Benjamin teased as he walked out of the room. "Bell, what's going on?" I asked.

"Sit." Bell said. I walked over and sat in the other chair across from Bell. "Is it true? Is what Caleb and the others saying true?" I asked. "Yes." Bell replied. "There is a prophecy about a vampire who can indeed have children. However, the children of course are born vampires. Which would make them purebloods." Bell explained.

"Why me? Why do I have to be the one to have the dreams?" I asked. "Because its your gift." Bell replied. I didn't know what to say. I couldn't even think of what to say I was in so much shock. In that moment Eve entered the room. "We are ready to go when you are." Eve said. "We will be right down." Bell replied. "We will be waiting." Eve said.

As Eve left the room I started to speak to Bell again. "I don't understand any of this." I said. "I know. Its quite confusing. Right now we need to get to Astarte so we can take care of Jade and then find Julian." Bell replied. I nodded and got up out of the chair and followed Bell out of the room.

As Bell and I walked passed the other rooms we saw that the others had went down stairs. When we got to the room at the end of the hall we saw everyone standing there waiting. Including the siblings. "Our flight leaves at ten." Lex said. "Let's get going." Athena said. "Joseph?" William called. "Yes my lord?" Joseph said. "take care of the house while we're gone." William said.

"Yes sir," As we walked out of the room and out into the cold there was only one thing going through my mind. Ashley. I knew that I had to keep her safe at any cost. She was my best friend. I couldn't let her down. I had to stop Jade. I wasn't as worried about stopping Jade as I was about Julian.

I wondered what was going to happen when we reached Egypt. Would Julian be merciful? Would he kill us all as soon as we stepped on the sands? What would Julian do to us? These were the thoughts that were running through my mind.

Was Mary leading us all to our deaths? Hell, was she even telling us the truth? Many thoughts came to mind as we headed to the airport. We had quite a journey a head of us. There was no turning back now. We had all come to far. There was no way that I was going to run. I would stand and fight until the end. Even if the end was my own.

Chapter 7

Visiting The Past

As we walked through the crowded streets of Ireland I remembered the feeling I had when I was going on trial before Astarte. I was nervous last time that I came here but I wasn't nervous this time. This time I felt as if I was coming to visit an old friend. I knew I had no reason to fear Astarte or expect the worst. He was a kind and gentle man. Even though he was one of us. I was more than happy to be going into his domain.

"Do you think that Astarte will help us?" Lex asked. "I'm certain of it." I replied. "Astarte is a very fair man. He will listen to all sides before making his decision." Caleb said. "I hope your right." William said. "Do not doubt our father." Athena said. "Astarte has been a good king.

He is the greatest that there ever was." Athena added. "I did not mean to offend you sister." William replied. "Let's just get to Astarte's castle and fight later." Athena said. As I walked toward Astarte's castle with the others I saw all of the humans on the side of the street looking at me as they had when I came to Ireland before.

"Caleb?" I said. "What?" Caleb said as he looked over at me. "These humans are looking at me the same way that they did when we came here before." I replied. "They do that. Humans tend to stare at things that amaze them." Caleb explained. "Well I wish they would stop." Caleb started to laugh.

"That's not going to happen." As we walked through the woods and came near the castle everything looked the same. The torches were still lit. There was still two guards at the entrance to the castle. Everything still looked the same. It was as if none of it had ever changed at all.

"We are here to see Astarte." Bell said. "Enter." One of the guards replied. As we entered the castle Ashley looked around as if she was stunned in amazement. "Wow. This place is huge." Ashley said as she continued to look around. "This is Astarte's castle." Amelia said.

"Your going to love Astarte. He's so cool." Alyssa told Mason. "He has to be cool to have a big castle like this." Mason replied. "I wonder if Astarte will remember me." Mary said. "I'm sure he will. Astarte remembers all of his children." Caleb replied.

As we walked down the stairs and entered the main room Astarte walked over to greet us. Pandora and the others remained seated in their chairs behind the table. "I knew I smelled company." Astarte said as he walked over toward us. "Elizabeth, it is so good to see you my child." Astarte said as he leaned over to hug me.

"You too." I replied. "Caleb, Amelia, oh your all here. What a pleasant surprise." Pandora said, "Hello Pandora." Amelia said. "Mommy!" Sky yelled as she jumped down from Pandora's lap and ran toward Raven.

"Oh my sweet little girl. How I've missed you" Raven said as she knelt down to hug Sky. "I see you have brought some new friends with you Caleb." Astarte said. "Yes. We have came together under some unfortunate circumstances." Caleb replied. "What's wrong?" Astarte asked.

"Jade attacked us on the way here. She's after Ashley. Elizabeth's friend." Caleb explained. "Who's Ashley?" Pandora asked. "That would be me." Ashley said as she stepped out from behind Amelia.

"Another human." Connor said shaking his head. Rosemary nudged him in the arm. "Elizabeth has a habit of getting involved with humans." Beth said. "I knew Ashley before I was turned. She's not just any human." I replied. "I see." Beth said.

"Have you come to ask us to help you fight Jade?" Phillip asked. "Yes." Darren said. "As you can see we have enlisted some help already. We could use all the help we can get." I said. "Its not just Jade that we have to worry about." Mary said.

"Mary? I haven't seen you in a long time. I thought that was you." Astarte said. "What else is going on?" Rosemary asked. "Would you like to do the honors Mary?" I asked as I looked at her with a devious smile. "After all it is your problem." I added in a harsh tone of voice.

"Certainly." Mary replied. "Julian has my husband Bradley." Astarte looked at Mary with wide eyes. "Julian?" Astarte asked. "Yes." Shane said. "Why is Julian after you?" Astarte asked. "Here comes the good part." I said with a slight grin. Caleb nudged me in the arm.

Darren started to laugh. "Hush." Amelia whispered as she nudged Darren in the arm. "I made the mistake of taking something very valuable from Julian. In return he took Bradley from me only to hold him hostage until I bring him back what I took." Mary explained.

"What did you take from Julian?" Astarte asked. "A potion. Its made of Julian's blood. It allows a vampire who is not pureblooded to be able to walk into the sunlight forever." Mary replied. "That's really possible?" Connor asked. "Yes it is." Shane replied. "If we all work together we can bring down Jade as well as Julian and his family." Bell said. "Will you help us?" I asked.

Astarte turned around to look back at his family. They all nodded in agreement. Even Connor surprisingly. "We will help you." Astarte replied. "I have no intention of giving this potion back to Julian. Once I am reunited with my husband he and I will drink the potion and walk off into the sunlight together forever." Mary said.

"Any of you who want to join us in the sunlight may drink from the potion as well. Julian keeps many bottles of it under lock and key in his castle." Mary added. "We will definitely need to get those bottles then." Lex said. "We want to experience the joy of the sunlight as well." Eve said.

"As do my family and I." Pandora said. "Agreed then. "If you all help me get my husband back then you can all have that joy once again." Mary said. "Agreed." Phillip said. "You may all stay in the guest quarters." Astarte said. "Caleb and his family can show you all where they are. They have been here before." Astarte added.

"Yes it has been a long trip. My family and I could use some rest." William replied. "Follow us." Caleb said. "There's only four guest rooms so we're going to have to cram together." Victor said. "That's alright. My family and I can stay in one room." Lex replied.

"Ok. Then Elizabeth, Amelia, Star, and my brothers can stay in the next room while Bell, Benjamin, Mason, and Alyssa stay in the middle room and Raven, Sky, Mary, and Shane can stay in the last room." Caleb said. "Who do you want to room with Ashley?" I asked.

"I think I'll just room with Raven if that's ok." Ashley replied with a light smile as she looked over at Shane. "Fine with me." Raven said. Shane began to smile. "Alright." Caleb said. "Raven, keep Shane away from Ashley. Please." I said as I gave Shane an evil glare.

"Will do." Raven replied as she took Sky's hand and started walking toward the room. "Let's head to our rooms then." Amelia said. "We will fly out to Pensacola tomorrow night. I will have Phillip make the arrangements." Astarte said.

"Oh by the way there are two beds in each room. You shouldn't have to cram together too much." Astarte added. "Thank you." Mary replied. As we headed to our rooms I felt relieved. I was ready to get some sleep. I knew that things would get tough when we got back to Pensacola.

I knew that Jade would be there waiting for us to return. She wasn't stupid enough to follow us to Astarte's castle. At least not after having to fight all of us back in Alaska.

As soon as Caleb and I got into our room with the others I sat down on the bed. "Well brother, I guess since there are only two beds you and Victor can sleep in one while I sleep in other one with the girls." Darren teased. "In your dreams Darren." I replied.

Amelia and Star started to laugh. "Well that was cold." Darren said. "Oh you'll get over it." Amelia said as she leaned over to kiss Darren on the cheek. Now Caleb and Victor started to laugh. "That's not funny." Darren said as he gave Caleb and Victor an evil glare. "Yes it is." Victor replied. "Huh." Darren said as he crossed his arms and looked away.

We all couldn't help but to laugh. We loved picking on Darren as much as he loved to pick on all of us. While the others and I were having fun picking on Darren things were beginning to get warmed up between Ashley and Shane. "Ashley would you like to share a bed with me?" Mary asked.

"Sure." Ashley replied. "I just thought I would ask since Raven would be sharing the other bed with her daughter." Mary said. "That's fine." Ashley said as she sat down on the bed. "Here's an extra blanket. I'm sure your still freezing from the trip to Alaska." Raven said. "Thank yyou."

"Where are you going to sleep Shane?" Ashley asked. "On the floor." Shane replied. "Your more than welcome to join me." Shane said with a big smile. "Forget it." Raven said. "Oh yes I forgot, Elizabeth makes all the rules now." Shane as he winked over at Ashley.

"No she doesn't." Ashley said as she curled up under the blanket. "Elizabeth only wants to keep Ashley away from you and your devious tactics." Raven said. "Oh I'm so hurt." Shane replied in a sarcastic voice. "Knock it off Shane." Mary said.

"Yes mother." Shane said as he laid down on the floor. "Ashley?" Mary said as she sat down on the bed. "Yes?" Ashley said as she pulled the blanket up to her chin trying to get warm. "How long have you known Elizabeth?" Mary asked. "Not long." Ashley replied. "We were roommates in college." Ashley added. "What's she like?" Mary asked. "Simple. She's not like most girls."

"Did you know the woman that took care of her?" Mary asked. "Yes. Mrs. Cromwell was a very nice woman. She was a very kind hearted person. There was no one like her." Ashley replied. "I can believe that. She was nice enough to take Elizabeth in." Mary said as she started to look sad. "Mary?" Raven said. "Yes?" Mary said as she looked over at Raven. "I know its not any of my business, but out of curiosity why did you give Elizabeth up?" Raven asked.

"After Elizabeth's father died I was lost. I didn't want to live anymore. It was like I had lost my best friend." Mary replied. "I wanted Elizabeth to have a good life. I didn't want her to live life without a father much less a mother who had become incapable of loving. She didn't deserve that." Mary added. Mary looked as if she was hiding something. Like she wasn't telling the whole truth.

"I guess I can understand that then." Raven replied. "Yes but Elizabeth may never understand that." Ashley said. "When all of this is over maybe we can try to make her understand." Raven suggested. "Maybe." Mary replied. "You three are killing me with the chick talk. I'm going for a walk." Shane said as he got up off the floor.

"Would you like to come?" Shane asked as he turned to look at Ashley. Before Ashley could say anything Raven began to speak. "No she wouldn't." Raven said. "We'll I'll be back in a little while." Shane replied as he turned and walked out of the room.

"I think my son has fallen in love with you." Mary said. "I'm also sensing that the feeling is mutual." Mary added. "Yeah. It is." Ashley admitted as she started to blush. While Ashley and Mary talked about Shane I decided to go outside for some fresh air.

"Where are you going?" Caleb asked as I got up off the bed. "I'm going outside for a little bit. I'll be back in a few minutes." I replied. "Don't get lost out there." Darren teased. I hit Darren on the arm as I walked toward the door.

As I walked down the hallway I saw Bell standing outside of her room. She was leaning against the wall with her arms crossed. "Shane's outside. Be nice to him. He's not really as bad as you think." Bell said. "Yeah. I'll keep that in mind." I replied. "What are you doing out here in the hallway." I asked.

"Just thinking. Benjamin's asleep." I replied. "I thought that I would step out here and take a load off." Bell teased. "Well have fun with that. I'm going outside." As I walked down the hall and headed outside I felt like something was about to happen that I wouldn't have expected. Something that would catch me off guard. If I had learned anything in the past it was to go with my feelings.

My feelings had always lead me to the truth. They even lead me to where I needed to be. I wondered what was going to happen when I stepped outside and saw Shane. I wondered if we would get along or if we would try to kill each other. Now that I think about it killing him wouldn't be a bad idea. It would kind of be a relief. At least I wouldn't have to listen to his annoying voice. However, I knew that deep down inside I couldn't kill him. Whether I liked it or not he was my brother.

He was half of me. Just like is Alyssa is half to me. I guess whether I like it or not I have to put up with Shane. Especially after the dreams that I had I know that I have to put up with him for Ashley's sake. Little did my best friend know she was about to become one of us as well as carry my brother's child. This was one family affair from hell.

Chapter 8

Making Up For Lost Time

As I stepped outside looking into the beauty of the night onceagain I saw Shane standing over by a tree. He was looking up at the moon as if he was thinking hard about something. As I walked slowly toward him he turned around to speak. It was as if he had been expecting me to show up. Here we go I thougt.

"I suppose your hear to give me grief?" Shane asked. "No. I just came out here to do some thinking." I replied. "About what?" Shane asked. "Jade, Julian, but most importantly Ashley." In that moment Shane looked at me with a look that I had never seen before as I mentioned Ashley's name. "I know that Ashley is your friend Elizabeth and I would never do anything to harm her. I hope you believe that."

"I know you wouldn't." I replied. "I love Ashley." Shane continued. "I know that her and I just have met and I know that you have just had a rough experience with having to deal with the fact that I'm your brother but I hope that you and I can get along because I really do love Ashley." This was not the conversation that I was expecting to have with Shane but I decided to go with it.

"Shane there's something that you should know." I said as I turned to face him. "What?" Shane asked. "I've been known to dream about the future. I had a dream about you and Ashley." I replied.

"What happened?" Shane asked looking worried. I wanted to tell him about how I saw Ashley carrying his child in the dream but I figured I would just let that be for now and just tell him about how I saw her becoming one of us. "Ashley will become one of us and you and her will be together."

" I take it by the look in your eyes you don't want her to become one of us." Shane said as he looked at me with sadness in his eyes. "Would you?" I asked. Shane looked at me as if he understood where I was going with this. "I get your point. It's not as great as it may seem to be one of us." Shane replied.

"I won't force Ashley to become one of us. Not if she doesn't want to." Shane added. "I know you wouldn't." I replied. "Elizabeth, the only way that I would ever turn Ashley into one of us is if she wanted to be with me. I would never force that kind of choice on her."

"Bell is right. Your not as bad as I thought." I said with a slight grin. "Yeah. Your not so bad yourself." Shane replied as he smiled back at me. "Elizabeth I know that none of this has been easy for you. I don't expect you to consider me as your brother. At least not if you don't want to." Shane added.

"Shane you are my brother and it has been a rough road but everything happens for a reason. Maybe one day you can consider me as your sister." I replied. "I already do." Shane said as he leaned forward to hug me. "Even though you are in pain." Shane teased.

"Yeah, yeah." I said as I punched him in the arm. "We better get back inside and get some rest. We got a long night ahead of us tomorrow." I said as I pulled away. "Yeah we do." Shane replied.

"Come on." As Shane and I walked back inside the castle I was beginning to feel as if I had done something good. I felt as if I had finally fixed the broken bridge between Shane and I. It was time to put the past behind us and concentrate on the future.

We had all come to far to let the past stop us now. It was time to make matters into our hands. As I walked into the room I saw that everyone was asleep except for Caleb. He was sitting on the bed with his arms crossed looking up at me. "Did you get some fresh air?" Caleb asked with a smile on his face.

"Yes along with other things." I replied as I laid down next to him. "What other things?" Caleb asked. "I talked to Shane while I was outside." I replied. "How did that go? Is he still in one piece?" Caleb asked looking worried. "Yes." I replied with a laugh. "He's not as bad as he seems." I added. "Well I'm glad you two are getting along." Caleb replied.

"Me too." I said as I laid my head on Caleb's chest. "Let's get some sleep. Tomorrow is going to be rough." Caleb said. "Yes it is." As I slept I dreamed about the little baby boy that I saw in the field. Only this time he was older. He looked as if he was five. I was standing in the same field that I had dreamed about before.

It was sunny. I was standing in the field in a long white dress. Everything still looked the same. The flowers, the waterfall, all of it. The little boy was running toward me with a hand full of flowers. As he came up to me I knelt down to look at him. He was so beautiful.

As the little boy reached out to give me the flowers he spoke. His voice was so beautiful. "Here you go mommy." The little boy said. As I reached out to take the flowers the little boy ran off down the field laughing. I started to laugh as I ran after him. It was like I was in heaven or something like it.

It was in that moment that I woke up and realized that it was night again. As I looked around I saw that I was the only one in the room and that everyone was gone. As I went to get up off of the bed I saw Bell standing in the door way.

"Hello sleepy head." Bell teased. "Hey." I replied. "Where is everybody?" I asked. "Everyone is down stairs. Astarte has called a meeting." Bell replied. "Alright lets go." As Bell and I walked down the hallway to the main room I wondered what was going on now. It was in the moment of that thought that Bell spoke.

"Astarte needs to get all of us together in order to go over the game plans." Bell said. "For what?" I asked. "For Jade and Julian." Bell replied. "We really do have our work cut out for us this time." I said as I kept walking down the hallway. "Yes we do." As Bell and I entered the main room I saw everyone gathered around the table where Astarte and his family were sitting.

"The dead has risen." Darren teased. Everyone started to laugh. "Yeah, yeah." I replied. "So what's our game plan?" I asked as I looked over at Astarte.

"Well we clearly we have a lot to deal with. I think that we may have to split up in order to take care of everything." Astarte replied. "What do you mean?" I asked. "Jade is trying her best to get to Ashley as well as you. I think that my family and I should go back to Pensacola with Bell and Benjamin to track Jade while you and the others go to Egypt and deal with Julian." Astarte explained. "I don't know if that's a good idea." Caleb said. "Why?" Astarte asked.

"Well what if that's what Jade wants? What if she's trying to split us up in order to get to Ashley?" Caleb asked. "That's a good point." Bell said. "Jade will follow us wherever we go as long as we have Ashley." Raven said. "I think the best thing that we can do is stay together." Amelia said.

"I agree." Lex said. "Alright then. We will go to Egypt and deal with Julian. I will arrange a flight there. We will leave at ten. In the mean time I suggest that you all feed and get your strength. Julian and his family are not to be taken lightly. They are just strong as they are deadly." Astarte said.

"Agreed." Victor said. "Let's go hunting. I'm hungry." Mason said. "Can I come watch?" Ashley asked. "Absolutely not." I replied. "Why?" Ashley asked. "Its dangerous for a human to be around us when we feed. We can lose control very easily. You could get hurt." I explained.

"We will take turns hunting so that Ashley is protected at all times. My family and I will go hunting first." Astarte said. "Alyssa and I will go with you." Mason said. "Shane and I will go with Bell and Benjamin." Mary said. "Actually I don't need to feed. I'll stay here with Ashley while you all go hunting." Shane replied. "Are you sure?" I asked. "Yeah. Don't worry Ashley will be alright."

"Are you ok with that Ashley?" Raven asked. "Yeah. I'll be fine."

Ashley replied. "Alright everyone lets go." Astarte said. As I walked out of the room with the others I knew that things were about to get pretty intense between Shane and Ashley. "Thanks for looking out for me. Its really sweet of you." Ashley said.

"No problem." Shane replied. "So what do you want to do while we wait for the others to get back?" Ashley asked. "I don't know." Shane replied. "What do you want to do?" Shane asked.

"Something fun." Ashley replied with a slight grin." I know just the thing. Come with me." Shane replied. "Where are we going?" Ashley asked. "Outside." Shane said as he took Ashley's hand into his and walked out of the room. When Shane and Ashley got outside they stood back behind the castle. They were standing in the middle of the garden when Shane started to speak again. "Close your eyes." Shane said.

As Ashley closed her eyes Shane put his arms around her waist and pulled her toward him. "What are you doing?" Ashley asked as she kept her eyes closed. "You'll see." Shane replied as he closed his eyes and kept his arms wrapped around Ashley. After a moment Shane began to float up into the air holding Ashley in his arms.

He began to fly over the castle and out toward the woods. He flew out near a field that was full of flowers. Across the field was a waterfall and a lake. It looked just like the place that I had seen in my dream. Shane flew down toward it and landed down in the center of the field.

After a moment he spoke again. "You can open your eyes now." As Ashley opened her eyes she looked around as if she was in shock. "Where are we?" Ashley asked. "In one of the most beautiful places in the world. "Shane replied. Ashley began to walk around as if she was stunned.

"Its amazing." Ashley said as she kept looking around. "Yes it is." Shane replied. "Have you ever brought anyone here before?" Ashley asked as she kept glancing around the place. "No." Ashley turned around to look at Shane in amazement. "Then why did you bring me here?" Ashley asked looking curious. "Because your special." Shane replied as he moved toward Ashley.

"Why?" Shane took a deep breath and began to speak again. "Ashley I need to tell you something." Ashley looked as if she was nervous. "Ok." Ashley said in a nervous voice.

"I have feelings for you that I've never had for anyone." Shane said. "I know what you mean." Ashley replied. "You do?" Shane asked as he moved closer. "Yes. I have feelings for you too." Shane looked as if he was surprised. "I love you Ashley." Shane said. "I love you too." Ashley replied as she leaned forward to kiss Shane.

"I want to be with you forever but I don't want to force the idea of eternity on you." Ashley put her finger on Shane's lips. "Shane I want to be with you. I would be more than happy to give up my life and follow you into eternity just to be with you." Ashley replied.

"Then its settled. When all of this is over you will become one of us." Shane said as he leaned in to kiss Ashley. While things were getting warmed up between Ashley and Shane things were about to get rough for the rest of us. As I followed behind Caleb and the others I could hear someone following close behind us. As I turned around to see who it was everyone else stopped walking and stood behind me looking off in the same direction.

There was no one to be seen but I knew that someone was out there. "Jade's close." Bell said. "Yes I know." I replied. "She's not going to attack us. She's not that stupid. There's too many of us." Connor said. "She's not alone." Bell replied. "Your right. I smell newborns." Astarte said.

"Everyone stay close together and keep your eyes open." I said as I walked out into the clearing of the woods. "Come out Jade! I know you're here!" I yelled. In that moment Jade was standing in front of me with ten newborns behind her. "Your getting pretty good with your senses." Jade said. One of the newborns looked at me as if she was simply disgusted with me. She had long black hair and the brightest golden eyes that I have never seen in my life.

"You need improvement on making surprise attacks." I said with a slight smile. "Well I would love to stand around and debate battle strategy with you but its time for you to die." Jade replied as she smiled back at me. "Attack!" Jade yelled.

As the newborns ran passed us I ran toward Jade and began to attack. The newborn with the long black hair ran toward me as if she was protecting Jade. I grabbed her and threw her back to the side.

While I was fighting Jade the others took on the newborns. I grabbed Jade and knocked her back into a tree. She got up after a moment and ran toward me and pushed me back so hard that I slid back across the ground.

I laid on the ground covered in dirt trying to get back up. As I laid there looking helpless Jade began to walk toward me. When she got over to where I was she knelt down and grabbed me by my hair and slowly pulled me up toward her.

"You know this has been fun. It's a shame that I have to kill you." Jade said. As Jade put her hand around my throat I began to feel severe amounts of pressure squeezing the life out of me. I thought this was it.

I thought that it was all over. In the moment of that thought Bell ran up and kicked Jade across the clearing. As I fell back toward the ground I saw Bell holding Jade by the throat.

"The only person who is going to die here is you. This is for my friend that you killed so very long ago." Bell said as she began to rip Jade's head off. Bell pulled Jade's head completely off of her body. As Jade's body fell to the ground Bell threw her head down next to it.

I felt relieved that Bell had finally gotten her revenge against Jade. As I looked over I saw that Caleb and the others had killed all of the newborns except one. The woman with the long black hair was missing. I guess she ran off to save herself. As I went to get up Bell ran over toward me.

"Are you alright?" Bell asked. "Yeah. You saved my life." I replied. "What are friends for." Bell replied with a slight smile. "We need to get rid off the bodies." Astarte said.

"Let's burn these animals." Connor said. "Lets stack them in a pile and burn them. It will be like a bonfire." Rosemary said in an excited voice. "You are so devious." Beth said as she looked over at Rosemary and crossed her arms. "Thank you." Rosemary replied with a smile. I stood back against a tree watching as Astarte and his family stacked the bodies in a pile to burn them.

"Well I see you got down and dirty." Caleb teased as he walked up toward. "Sometimes you have to fight dirty." I replied with a smile. "Well at least Jade's out of the picture." Caleb said as he put his arm around me. "Yeah. It must hurt you to see her gone." I replied as I laid my head on Caleb's shoulder. "No. The Jade I knew died a long time ago."

"This is the last one." Phillip said as he put the last body on the pile. "Light it." Astarte said as he looked over at Connor. As the bodies burned I felt relieved. I was glad that one of our problems had been solved.

As I looked across the bonfire I saw Bell sitting on the ground with tears of blood falling down her face. Benjamin stood beside her watching the fire burn while the others stood around the fire cheering about our victory. "I need to talk to Bell." I said as I leaned up and looked at Caleb. "Alright." Caleb replied. As I walked toward Bell she looked as if she was in a trance. There seemed to be a look of relief followed by unbearable pain on her face.

"Are you alright?" I asked as I sat down next to Bell. "Yeah. I'm just thinking about Anne." Bell replied. "She must have been a really good friend." I said as I put my arm around Bell. "She was. Anne was my best friend. The closest thing that I ever had to a sister." Bell said as she wiped the tears off of her face. "Well its over now. Jade is dead. You can finally take comfort in that thought and your friend can finally rest in peace." I replied.

"Thank you for being my friend Elizabeth. Your like a sister to me." Bell said as she leaned over and put her head on my shoulder. "Your welcome." I sat there with Bell as we watched the bodies burn to ash. After an hour it was time for us to head to the airport.

We started heading back to the castle to get Shane and Ashley. I wondered what they had been up to since we left. I wondered if they had been getting along. I figured they were getting along ok since I knew that Shane was in love with Ashley and the feeling was mutual. It was still hard knowing that Ashley was going to become one of us.

I didn't want her to give up her life. Ashley was young and still had a lot of life left to live.

I guess I felt that way because I didn't get to live mine. When we reached the castle I saw Shane and Ashley standing outside. They looked as if they had been waiting for us. "Elizabeth what happened? Your all covered in dirt." Ashley said as she walked over to look at me.

"Jade attacked with some newborns?" I replied.

"What?" Shane said as he walked over to check on me. "Mother are you ok?" Shane asked. "Yes son. I'm fine." Mary replied. "Where are they?" Ashley asked. "Dead." Benjamin replied. "I killed Jade." Bell said. "Its about time." Raven replied. "We killed all of the newborns and burned them along with Jade." Pandora said.

"Well at least we have one problem eliminated." Ashley said. "Its almost ten. We need to get to the airport." Astarte said. "I need to change clothes first. I'll be right back." I told them. "I'll come with you." Bell said. As I walked down the hall toward the room I started to feel a little dizzy.

"Are you alright?" Bell asked. "Yeah. I just feel a little dizzy." I replied. "Dizzy?" Bell said in disbelief. "Elizabeth you shouldn't be feeling dizzy you're a vampire." Bell added. "I know. I don't understand it either."

When I got in the room I walked over to the closet and grabbed my bag. As I walked over toward the bed I started to feel weak." Bell lifted me up and put me on the bed.

"Just sit on the bed for a minute." Bell said. "I don't know whats happening to me." I said as I put my hand on my head. In that moment Bell looked as if she was in a trance. She looked like she was having a vision. "I think I do." Bell said in a low voice. "What?" I said as I looked over at Bell. "Nothing."

I opened my bag and took out another pair of jeans and a black sweater. "I'll go stand outside while you change." Bell said. "Ok." As Bell closed the door behind her I stood up slowly and started to change clothes.

After I put on my new clothes I put the old ones in a bag so that the dirt wouldn't get everywhere. I walked over and put my bag back in the closet. I began to feel dizzy again. When I opened the door I saw Bell standing against the wall in the hall.

"Are you ready?" Bell asked. "Yeah." I replied. As we walked down the hall once again Bell looked as if she knew something. "Is something wrong?" I asked looking worried. "No." Bell replied.

When we got outside everyone was waiting for us. "Lets go." I said as I walked toward Caleb. As I walked through the woods with the others I began to feel even more dizzy.

"Wow." I said as I almost fell over on the ground. "Elizabeth?" Caleb said as he came over to hold me up. "Are you alright?" Caleb asked. "Yeah." I replied. Amelia and Bell looked at each other as if they knew something. Amelia began to smile.

I had no idea what was going on but I knew that something was wrong. Something was going on right under my nose and it was only a matter of time before it floated up to the surface. "You don't look so well." Caleb said worried. "I'm fine." Bell definitely looked as if she was hiding something. I knew that there was something that she wasn't telling me.

It was obvious by the look on her face that I was right. Something was going on and she knew it. I couldn't understand why she wasn't telling me what was going on but if I knew Bell she had a reason for being mysterious. It was only a matter of time before I found out the truth.

Chapter 9

Egypt

As we sat on the plane waiting to reach Egypt I began to feel like I was on fire. My stomach felt as if it had become unsettled. I knew something was wrong now. I was having feelings that a vampire shouldn't be having. What's happening to me? I thought. In the moment of that thought Bell looked over at me. She looked at me with a slight grin on her face. I looked at her confused. Why would Bell be smiling? I thought. After a moment she turned back to look at Benjamin. I knew something weird was going on now.

"Are you alright?" Caleb asked looking worried again. "I don't know. I don't feel so well." I replied. Caleb reached out to put his hand on my cheek. "Well this is strange." Caleb said as he ran his hand down my face. "What is it?" I asked worried.

"Your burning up. Something is wrong. Its not normal for vampires to be like this." Caleb replied. "When we get to Egypt I'm going to have Bell look at you. She has a good medical back ground. She will know what to do." Caleb added. "She knows something that's for sure." I replied.

"Just try to relax. We will be landing soon." I did as Caleb said and I closed my eyes and tried to relax. It was a long shot though. Every time I tried to relax I would start to feel worse. It wasn't long after that when the plane landed. As soon as it did I was relieved.

When I got off the plane I started to feel dizzy again. As I tried to walk toward the gates I began to stumble. "Elizabeth?" Caleb said as he grabbed my arm. "She's really weak. We need to get her somewhere she can rest." Bell said as she put her hand on my forehead.

"She's burning up." Bell said in a worried voice. "That's not normal." Benjamin said. In that moment I passed out. "Elizabeth!" Caleb said in a panic. "She's ok. She just passed out." Bell said. "What's wrong with her?" Alyssa asked. "What happened?" Mary asked as she walked up behind us.

"There's no easy way to say this. I think that Elizabeth is with child." Bell replied. "What?" Mary said in disbelief. "That's impossible. She's not hybrid." Shane said. "Its not impossible if Elizabeth is the vampire from the prophecy and I think she is." Bell replied.

"Prophecy? What prophecy?" Mary asked. "There's a prophecy about a vampire who can conceive children with other vampires." Amelia replied. "All the things that are happening to Elizabeth are signs of vampire pregnancy as we call it." Bell said. "Well this is wonderful." Shane said in a sarcastic voice.

"I know a place where she can rest." Astarte said. "Where?" Caleb asked. "There's a temple not far from here. Its right outside of Egypt." Astarte replied. "Take us there." Darren said.

As Caleb followed Astarte with the others toward the temple I was unconscious and in a whole other world. It was in that time that I dreamed once again. My mother appeared to me once more. "Elizabeth?" My mother said. She was standing in the woods in a long white dress.

"Mother?" I said as I stood in the middle of the clearing looking back at her. "Yes. Your dreaming my dear." Mother replied. "I know." I said as I smiled and walked toward her to give her a hug. Mother felt so real to me.

"I've missed you so much." I said as I pulled away. "I've missed you too." Mother replied. "Mother I'm scared. Something is happening to me." Mother looked at me with a smile on her face. "There's nothing to be afraid of. Whats happening to you is a wonderful thing." Mother assured me. "What is happening to me?" I asked.

"A miracle. Something wonderful." Mother replied as she reached out to take my hand. "I don't understand." I said as I looked at my mother confused. "You will in time. Its time for you to wake up now." Mother replied. "You are terrible at reassurance." I teased.

Mother smiled and began to walk away. In that moment I woke up to see Caleb sitting in a chair next to me. "Welcome back." Caleb said as he reached out to put his hand on my forehead. "She's awake." Amelia said as she stepped outside of the doorway to tell the others. Alyssa and Mason entered the room.

"How do you feel?" Alyssa asked. "Ok I guess." I replied as I woke up. The room that I was in had golden walls with Egyptian symbols all over them. "I had another dream about mom." I added. "That's nice." Alyssa said as she rubbed her hand on my forehead. "Get some rest." Mason said. "I cant take on Julian and his siblings by myself." Mason teased.

I looked back at him with a slight grin on my face. In that moment Mary and Shane entered the room with Ashley. "I'll leave you all to talk." Alyssa said. Amelia put her arm around Alyssa as Mason followed behind them out of the room.

"How are you doing?" Mary asked. "I'm alright." I replied. "It's good to have you back with us." Shane said. "It's good to be back." I said with a big smile. "Get some rest. You will need your strength when we face Julian." Mary said. "Come on. She needs her rest." Shane said as he put his hand on Mary's shoulder and turned to walk out of the room.

"Could you all give me a moment alone with Elizabeth? I need to speak to her." Ashley said. "Of course." Caleb replied. As Caleb walked out of the room with Shane and Mary I wondered what Ashley was going to say to me.

She came over and sat in the chair next to the bed and began to speak. "Why are you fighting so hard to protect me?" Ashley asked. "Because you're my friend." I replied. "Friends protect each other and they stand by each other when there's trouble." I added.

"I appreciate everything that your doing but look at what protecting me has done to you." Ashley said as she reached out and put her hand on my forehead. "Whatever is going on with my body has nothing to do with you."

"It has to. You didn't start getting sick until I came into the picture." Ashley replied. "Stop it. This is not your fault." I assured her. "There's something wrong with me and I don't know what it is but I know that Bell and Amelia know what it is. Their too afraid to say anything." I added.

"That doesn't make any since." Ashley said in disbelief. "Why wouldn't they tell you?" Ashley asked looking confused. "I don't know but I'm going to find out." While Ashley and I continued our conversation the others stood outside of the room debating whether or not to tell me what was going on with me.

"She has got to know." Bell said. "Yes but not now." Astarte replied. "Why not?" Caleb asked. "Elizabeth needs to focus on the problem at hand." Connor replied. "It will take all of us to bring down Julian and his siblings." Phillip said. "That may be true but Elizabeth deserves to know the truth." Amelia said. "She is carrying my brothers child." Victor said.

"I understand your concern Victor but if Elizabeth finds out that she is pregnant then her focus will be lost." Astarte replied. "She will be concentrating too much on her unborn child and because of that she could put all of our lives at risk." Astarte explained. "So when are we suppose to tell her the truth?" Alyssa asked. "After we have defeated Julian." Connor replied.

"This seems rather cruel to put Elizabeth through all of this." Eve said. "I agree." Lex said. "Astarte, I trust you because my sister trusts you. She holds a very high respect for you and because of that so do I, but I promise you that if anything happens to my sister or her unborn child that she is carrying I will personally hold you responsible and make your life a living hell." Alyssa said.

Astarte smiled and walked toward her. "I wouldn't have it any other way." Astarte replied. "Nothing is going to happen to your sister." Pandora said. "She will be fine." Rosemary said.

"Let us hope so." Caleb replied. "Do you really think that she will be able to fight in her condition?" Mason asked. "Elizabeth is strong. She won't give birth for a while. A vampire pregnancy is a lot different from human pregnancy." Astarte replied.

"It takes two months for a vampire child to fully develop. Hybrids are different. It only takes a month for them to develop." Astarte explained. "I don't know why its like that. I never really understood the difference." Astarte added.

"She's not the only one that's expecting." Astarte continued. "What are you talking about?" Raven asked. "Ashley is pregnant." Astarte replied. "What?" Shane said in disbelief. "Yes. I had a vision of her being with child. Your going to be a father Shane." Astarte replied.

"No wonder you wanted to stay behind and look after her." Darren teased. Alyssa nudged Darren in the arm. "Why do I always get hit?" Darren said as he rubbed his arm. "Because its fun." Alyssa replied. "I'm going to be a grandma. Again." Mary said in excitement as she leaned over to hug Shane.

"I can't believe it." Shane said in disbelief. "Well believe it." Athena said. "Congratulations." William said. "I've got to tell Ashley." Shane replied. "I don't know if that's such a good idea right now." Star said.

"Yeah. You might send Ashle into shock and she's already in shock enough as it is with Elizabeth being sick." Bell said. "I'll wait a little while and then tell her when we're alone." Shane replied. "Good idea." Mary said.

"I'm going to be a father. I'm so happy!" Shane said in an excited voice. "When all of this is over I'm going to ask Ashley to be my wife." Shane added. "That will make her very happy." Alyssa replied. While everyone celebrated the happy moment Ashley was starting to come down with the same symptoms that I had.

"Are you alright?" I asked. "Yeah. I just feel a little dizzy." Ashley replied. "I guess something is just going around." Ashley said as she put her hand on her forehead. "Why would you be affected by it though?" Ashley asked. "I don't know. Maybe because your sick I can feel it." I replied.

"Maybe I've come into another power that I didn't know I had." I added. "Maybe so." Ashley replied. "I'm going to leave now and let you get some rest." Ashley added. "Alright." I said as I laid my head back and closed my eyes. When Ashley walked out of the room everyone stared at her. They were doing their best to hide the news from her.

"What's going on?" Ashley asked. "Nothing." Raven replied. "How's Elizabeth?" Shane asked. "She's ok. I left her to rest." Ashley replied. "Good. She needs all of the rest that she can get." Amelia said. "I think I have an idea on what's wrong with Elizabeth." Ashley said.

"You do?" Caleb asked. "Yeah. While I was in the room talking to her I started to feel dizzy. I think that Elizabeth may have came into another power that she didn't know she had." Ashley replied.

"What do you mean?" Darren asked. "I think that Elizabeth may be an empath. I think that I'm sick and she's feeling what I feel." Ashley replied. "Well that makes since." Shane said. "Ashley, can you and I go somewhere and talk?" Shane asked. "Sure." Ashley replied looking worried. "Is everything alright?" Ashley asked looking worried once more.

"Yeah. I just need to talk to you about something." Shane replied. "This is going to be good." Darren whispered. "Hush." Amelia whispered back. While Shane and Ashley went outside to talk the others stood outside of my room talking while I slept. As Ashley walked outside with Shane she began to worry about what it was that he had to tell her.

"You should sit down." Shane said. "Ok." Ashley said as she sat down on the steps in front of the temple. "There's something that you need to know and its going to be a shock." Shane said as he sat down next to Ashley on the steps. "Ok, what is it?" Ashley asked looking worried again.

Shane paused for a moment. He knew that he couldn't reveal the whole truth behind what Astarte had said but he knew that he could work his way around the truth by telling the part that involved Ashley.

"The reason why you got dizzy a while ago is because there's something going on with your body. Your not sick." Ashley looked at Shane with a worried look. "Then what's wrong with me?" Ashley asked.

"Your pregnant." Shane replied. "What?" Ashley said in disbelief. "I didn't know this before but according to Astarte hybrids can conceive children with humans." Shane replied. "Elizabeth has been sick because she has a new power. She can feel what your feeling." Shane lied. Shane hated having to lie to Ashley about me but he knew that Caleb would tell me the truth when the time was right.

"Well now it makes since." Ashley replied. "I'm going to have a baby." Ashley said with a slight grin as she reached out and put her arms around Shane's neck. "Are you happy? I mean is this what you want?" Shane asked. "Of course it is." Ashley replied as she leaned to kiss Shane.

"There's one more thing." Shane said. "What's that?" Ashley asked. Shane reached out and took Ashley's hand as he got down on one knee. "Ashley, will you be my wife?" Ashley sat there with her mouth open. She was completely speechless. She didn't know what to say. After a few moments Ashley spoke. "Yes."

Shane picked Ashley up and spun her around. They looked like the happiest couple in the world that moment. "Let's go tell the others." Ashley said. While Ashley and Shane went to tell the others their wonderful news I started to dream again. Only this time it wasn't about my mother. It was a nightmare.

I was standing in a room with walls made of stone along with stoned statues all around. They were Egyptian statues. There was no one in the room. I was the only one. After a moment I heard someone call my name. "Elizabeth?" The voice sounded like a man. As I turned around I saw a man with short dark hair and gold eyes. He has no shirt and was wearing dark jeans. He was a vampire by the smell of him.

The man looked as if he hadn't fed in weeks. He looked as if he had been tortured. "Who are you?" I asked. "Help me." The man replied.

"How?" I asked. "Help me before its too late." The man continued. "How?" I asked again looking confused.

In that moment the man began to scream. He looked as if he was in unbelievable pain. "Hold on I'm coming!" I yelled. As I ran toward the man his screams became louder and louder. Before I could get to him he turned into ash. I reached out and touched the ashes with my hand. In that moment I heard another voice.

"Elizabeth?" It sounded like Caleb's voice. "Wake up. Elizabeth?" In that moment I woke up to see Caleb standing over me. "Its time for us to go to Julian's castle." Caleb said. "Go get Mary. I need to talk to her." I replied. "What's wrong?" Caleb asked. "I'm not sure. I need to ask Mary some questions." Caleb walked out of the room and came back with Mary in a minute.

"What's going on?" Mary asked. "Do you know anything about a room with stoned walls and Egyptian statues all around it?" I asked. "Yes. That's Julian's castle. It's the room that he and his siblings stay in." Mary replied. "I dreamed about that room and a vampire that was in it."

"What did the vampire look like?" Mary asked. "He was tall with dark hair and gold eyes." I replied. "That's Bradley." Now the dream made since to me. "He looked tortured. He looked like he hadn't fed in weeks." I continued. "In the dream Bradley asked me to help him before it was too late and then he turned to ash." Mary looked at me with a worried face.

"If we don't hurry Julian will put Bradley out into the sun to burn." Mary replied as she ran her fingers through her hair. "Don't worry. We will stop Julian and get Bradley back." Caleb said. "We need to get going." I told them. "Before we go Ashley wants to tell you something." Caleb said.

"She can tell me on the way." I replied as I got up off of the bed. When I got outside of the room Ashley was standing in front of the others. "Caleb said that you had something that you needed to tell me." I said.

"Yes. I'm pregnant and Shane asked me to be his wife." Ashley replied as Shane walked up and put his arm around her. I couldn't believe it. Even more I couldn't understand how it was possible with Shane being half vampire.

"Congratulations." I said as I leaned forward to hug Ashley. "That's why you have been sick. You have a new power. You can feel what others feel." Ashley explained. "Well that makes a lot of since." I said relieved. "Yeah, don't worry though, the baby will be here in a month. You won't feel sick for long." Ashley teased.

"I'm so happy for you. I just hope that you realize what this means." I replied. "What are you talking about?" Ashley asked as her smile faded away. "What Elizabeth is trying to say is that she hopes that you understand the full weight of the decision that you have made." Shane said. "What do you mean?" Ashley asked looking confused.

"When the baby comes it will do a lot of damage to your body because it is half vampire." Caleb replied. "What are you saying?" Ashley asked looking worried. "You can't give birth to a hybrid child and live." Mary said. "In the end you will have to be changed into one of us." Mary added.

"If Shane changes you then you will be a hybrid like him. If any of us do it you will be a full vampire." Raven said. "So because I'm carrying a child that is half vampire the price that I've paid in the end is becoming one of you so that I can be around to raise my child?" Ashley asked. "Yes." Mary replied.

"So this is one of the reasons why you were so against me becoming like you?" Ashley asked as she looked over toward me. "Yes." I replied. "I understand where all of you are coming from but I can't undo what has already been done." Ashley replied.

"If this is the price that I must pay in order to be with Shane as well as to be able to have the joy of raising my child and being a mother than I accept it." Ashley added. "It's settled then. You will become one of us after you have your baby." I replied.

I couldn't believe the words were coming out of my mouth. I guess whether I liked it or not Ashley was going to become one of us. I guess you can't always chose your fate much less who shares it with you.

"We need to get to Julian's castle. We don't have much time." I told them. "I'll lead the way." Mary said. "Do you still have the potion?"

I asked. "Yes." Mary replied. "Good. Keep it on you. I have an idea." Everyone looked at me as if they were confused.

Amelia and Bell however looked as if they knew what I was doing. "What's our plan?" Caleb asked. "Does Julian have guards?" I asked. "Of course." Mary replied. "When we get to the castle I want you to tell the guards that you have come to return the potion to Julian. They will let you in without question."

"What about the rest of you?" Mary asked. "I will sneak in the castle from the back with the others. Eve and her family will come in from the west side while Connor, Rosemary, Beth and Phillip come in from the east side. Make sure and take out any guards that you see on your way in." I replied.

"My family and I will take them by surprise from behind while you, Shane, and Astarte come in from the front to distract Julian." I added. "Pandora will you stay here at the temple and guard the children?" I asked.

"Of course." Pandora replied. "I'm use to being the baby sitter." Pandora teased. "Benjamin and I can stay with Pandora for extra protection." Bell said. "Thank you." Astarte said. "Think nothing of it." Bell replied. "We're happy to help." Benjamin said.

"We need to get going." I told them. "What about me?" Ashley asked. "You should stay here with Bell and the others. You will be a lot safer than with us." I replied. "But---."

"You will be alright. Bell and the others will protect you." Shane said cutting Ashley off. "I know that but I want to help you." Ashley replied. "You can help me by staying here where you will be safe." Shane said as he put his hand on Ashley's cheek.

"I love you." Ashley said as she leaned forward to kiss Shane. "I love you too." Shane replied. "Promise me that you will come back in one piece." Ashley said as she out her hand on Shane's cheek. "I promise." Shane replied. "You and I will be together forever. Always." Shane added.

"Come on. We have no time to lose." Mary said. "We've got to get your father back." Mary added. Bell put her arm around Ashley to comfort her while Shane and I walked away with the others.

As we walked out of the castle and made our way toward Julian's castle Bell began to speak in order to help put Ashley's mind at ease. "Don't worry. He's coming back." Bell said. "How do you know that?" Ashley asked. "I can see the future." Bell replied. "So you see everything?" Ashley asked looking interested. "Yes."

"What all do you see?" Ashley asked hoping that Bell's reply would be one that she wanted to hear. "I see you and Shane having a future together. You will have a healthy son and you will be one of us." Bell replied. "Bell, is becoming one of you really as bad as Elizabeth says it is?" Ashley asked in a worried voice.

"Yes it is. When you become one of us you will not only be dead but you will have no soul." Ashley looked away as if she wished that she hadn't asked Bell that question. "Do you know who will turn me?" Ashley asked. "Yes." Bell replied.

"Who will turn me?" Ashley asked looking curious. "Shane." Ashley looked as if Bell's answer had no effect on her. It was as if she had expected Shane to be the one to turn her all along. "Well its pretty obvious." Pandora said as she watched Serenity and Sky playing with dolls as they sat on the floor.

"I figured since Shane and I are together now that he would be the one to do it." Ashley replied. "Smart girl." Benjamin said.

"What else is going to happen in the future?" Ashley asked. "Well there is another thing, but if I tell you then you must promise me that you will not say anything to Elizabeth." Ashley looked at Bell with curious and confusing eyes for a moment and then began to speak again. "I promise."

"The reason why Elizabeth was sick before you was because she is pregnant as well." Ashley looked at Bell in disbelief. "I didn't think that vampires could have children." Ashley said as she continued to look amazed. "We can't, but apparently some of us can." Bell replied.

"Elizabeth is able to conceive because she is the vampire from the prophecy." Bell added. "Prophecy?" Ashley asked looking confused once more. "There's a prophecy about a vampire who is able to conceive with other vampires." Pandora said. "How was I able to get pregnant if Shane is half vampire?" Ashley asked still looking confused.

"Because Shane is half human. Hybrids can have children with women because they are half human." Bell replied. "Well that makes more since." Ashley said. "Why are you keeping this from Elizabeth?" Ashley asked. "If Elizabeth knew the truth it would only distract her from the problem at hand." Bell replied. "Do you plan to tell her the truth?" Ashley asked. "Yes."

"Caleb is going to tell Elizabeth after Julian is taken care of." Pandora said. "I bet Elizabeth is going to be so happy." Ashley said as she put her hand on her stomach and smiled. "I think she will be more shock than surprised." Bell replied with a slight grin.

"What makes you think that?" Ashley asked. "I can see the future remember." Bell said as she looked at Ashley smiling once again. "Right." Ashley replied. "Everything is going to be ok. It has to be." Ashley added.

While Ashley waited for us to come back the others and I were getting close to Julian's castle. It was only a matter of time before we could reach it and claim our victory as well as get Bradley back so that Mary would be happy again.

I wasn't sure what we would find when we got to the castle or how things would go down but I knew that I had to help get Bradley out of Julian's grasp. After all he was Shane's father.

If Shane and I were going to have a relationship as siblings than I knew that I had to do this. I never thought that I would say this but Shane was starting to grow on me. I felt as if I had known him all of my life. It was clear to me as I approached the castle with the others that I had to do this. I couldn't help but to feel as if I was being a little selfish though.

I wanted to do this in order to help my brother and Mary but deep down I was doing it for my own selfish reasons. Deep down I wanted to take all of the potions out of Julian's castle and drink one along with Caleb, Alyssa, and the others. I wanted to be able to feel the sunlight again. I wanted to feel as normal as I possibly could.

It was a long shot I know but even though I would never be normal again I figured that I could at least have a simple pleasure that would make me feel not only a little normal but one that would make me feel human again. Even though I never would be. In the moment of that last thought Mary began to speak.

"We're here." As I stood with the others I saw a tall golden castle made out of stone with an Egyptian pyramid on each side. There was a guard in front of each pyramid and two more standing in front of the golden double doors that clearly gave entrance to the castle.

"Remember our plan." I told everyone. With those last words Eve and her family took the west side while Astarte's family took the east side. While Astarte walked toward the castle with Mary and Shane I went around back with the others. This was going to be one hell of a surprise attack.

Chapter 10

Julian

While the others and I worked our way in through the castle Astarte was putting his verbal talents to good use. "I am Astarte. I have come to see Julian." Astarte said. "Julian will be happy to see you." One of the guards replied. "The other two here however need no introduction. We know who they are and Julian has been expecting them." The guard added. "I know. That's why I'm here. A deal is a deal." Mary said. "Enter." The guard replied. As Mary entered the castle with Shane and Astarte the others and I were having a hard time getting through the guards. All of the guards were vampires of course.

We fought our way through ten guards as we entered the castle from the back. As we got closer to the throne room where Julian and his siblings were we had to go through more guards. We were almost there. While I fought with the others to get to Julian, Mary was placing Julian straight into our trap by distracting him with the potion until the others and I could get there to take him down.

"Hello Julian." Mary said. "Hello Mary. I was beginning to wonder on whether or not you were going to come back." Julian replied. "Well I'm here." Mary said. "Where's my father?" Shane asked.

"Eric, bring Bradley out." Julian said. "As you wish." Eric replied.

"Do you have the potion?" Julian asked. "Yes." Mary replied. "Give it to us." Melina said. "Not until I have my husband." Mary replied. In that moment Eric brought Bradley out. He looked like he hadn't fed in weeks. He looked as if he had been tortured. As Bradley fell to his knees in front of Mary she knelt down to put her arms around him.

"Oh my love. This is all my fault." Mary said as tears of blood ran down her face. "Its alright. At least we're together again." Bradley replied. "Now give me the potion." Julian said. "No. Don't give it to him he'll just kill you afterwards." Bradley said. "Its ok." Mary replied. "Trust me." Mary said as she stood up and walked over toward Julian with the potion in her hand. In that moment the others and I busted through the double doors from the back.

"No Mary don't!" I yelled. "Who is this?" Julian asked as he stood up looking outraged. "My name is Elizabeth." I said as I walked toward Mary. After a few minutes Eve and her family came in from the west side of the room. Shortly after Connor and the others came in from the east side.

We had Julian completely surrounded now. "What is the meaning of this?" Eric asked. "We have all come together to take you all down." I told them. "You want your potion back right?" Very well. You can have your potion and keep your worthless lives but Bradley comes free." I added.

"What makes you think that you have any power over me?" Julian asked. "You want your potion back don't you?" I asked with a slight smile on my face. "If I were you I would take the potion and go. Don't be stupid like Vladimir was." Caleb said.

"Was?" Julian asked. "Yes. I killed him." I replied. "You ruthless little harlot. He was my friend!" Julian said in an angry voice.

"Not anymore." I said as I smiled once again. "You will pay for his murder." Julian said. "Maybe you shouldn't have mentioned that." Mason said as he looked over toward me. "None of you will leave this castle alive!" Julian yelled.

"Guards!" Eric yelled. "Here we go again." Darren said. "Just like old times brother." Victor said as he began to smile. Twenty guards entered the room. We were all surrounded. "Get them!" Julian yelled.

"Mary! Shane! Go get the rest of the potions!" I yelled. "I won't leave Bradley!" Mary yelled back. "Don't worry I'll take care of him! Now go!" I yelled.

"Don't worry Mary. I'll go with you." Alyssa said. "I'm coming with you." Mason said as he followed behind Alyssa. As Mary and Shane fought through the guards and ran out of the room with Alyssa and Mason the rest of us continued to fight our way out.

"Darren! Amelia! Take Bradley and get out of here!" I yelled. Amelia and Darren ran toward Bradley. "Come on Bradley. We need to get you to safety." Amelia said. "I'll help." Raven said. Darren picked Bradley up and put him on his back and ran out of the room as Amelia and Raven followed.

After the others and I defeated the guards Julian and his siblings were the only ones who stood between us and the front door that we needed to get in order to get Mary and the others. "Connor, I want you and Phillip to take Rosemary and Beth out of here." Astarte said. "What about you?" Connor asked. "I'll be fine. Now go."

As Connor and the others ran out through the back doors I stood with the others waiting for Julian to attack. "The others may get out but you won't. You will all die." Julian first. "You first." I replied.

Julian grabbed a sword and ran toward me. Eric ran toward Lex and William while Eve and Athena took on Melina. Star began to attack Melina in order to help Eve and Athena while Caleb and Victor helped Lex and William. As usual I always took on the big bad dog by myself.

As Julian ran toward me I flipped over him and landed on the other side of the room causing him to miss. After a moment Julian turned around and began to run toward me once more.

This time I jumped up in the air and grabbed a sword off of the wall. While Julian and I began to clash swords the others were having a hard time fighting Melina and Eric. "You fools! You can't defeat us!" Eric yelled. While the others kept on fighting things were getting rough between Julian and I.

"I'm going to make sure that you have a slow and painful death before you meet Vladimir in hell." Julian said. "You won't live that long." I replied. Julian growled and ran toward me again. As I blocked his sword from hitting against me I kicked him back into one of the statues.

As the statues shattered Julian got up and came at me again. "This ends here!" Julian yelled. "I couldn't agree more." I replied. As Julian ran toward me holding his sword in the air preparing to strike I looked to the side of me and saw a spear. I picked it up and threw it toward Julian.

It only took a moment for the spear to pierce Julian's heart. As the spear went through Julian's body he fell to his knees. "No!" Melina yelled. The others looked at me as the fighting stopped. Julian's lifeless body was laying at my feet. "You will pay for this!" Melina yelled.

"No! Not now. Come with me sister." Eric said as he grabbed Melina by the arm. "This is far from over." Eric said as he looked over at me. "I'm counting on it." I replied. As Eric and Melina ran out through the doors behind us. The others and I ran toward the front door to meet up with Mary and the others.

As I ran down the hall with the others I saw Mary taking all of the potions off of the shelf in what looked to be like the supply room. Shane and Mason were holding potion bottles in their hands while Alyssa stood there keeping an eye out. "Elizabeth!" Alyssa yelled.

"What happened? Where is everyone?" Alyssa asked looking worried. "The others are waiting outside for us." I replied. "Where's Bradley?" Mary asked looking worried. "He's alright. Amelia and Darren are taking care of him." Caleb said.

"What about Julian and his family?" Shane asked. "Julian is dead and Eric and Melina ran off but they will be back." I replied. "I take it you killed Julian?" Mason asked. "What do you think?" I said with a slight grin on my face. "Yeah. Enough said." Mason replied.

"We need to get out of here and get back to the temple." I told them " I got all of the potions. We can all drink them when we get to the temple." Mary said. "Sounds good to me." Alyssa said. "Alright then. Let's go" I said as I started running down the hall. As the others and I ran out of the castle and headed toward the temple I began to have a bad feeling.

I began to feel worried about Bell and Pandora. I had a bad feeling that something was wrong. I started to worry about Ashley and wondered if she was still safe. I had a feeling once we made it to the temple that everything was going to change.

I felt as if there was something that was going to be waiting for us when we entered the temple and from the feeling I knew that it wasn't going to be good. "What's wrong?" Caleb asked as we got it outside and met up with the others. "I have a bad feeling about going back to the temple." I replied.

"Don't worry. I'm sure Bell and the others are fine." Caleb said. "I hope your right." I replied. "What happened?" Star asked. "Julian is dead and Eric and Melina will be back to take their revenge." I replied. "Well at least we have one of them out of the way." Darren said. "We need to get to the temple." Caleb said. As I walked with the others toward the temple I still had a feeling that something was wrong.

I couldn't be sure of what it was but I knew that something wasn't right. There was something about going back to the temple that didn't feel right to me. It only took us half an hour to get back to the temple. As we walked toward the doors the feeling that I had been having had gotten stronger.

As we entered the temple I saw that the room had been destroyed. "Bell! Pandora! I yelled. "Ashley!" Shane yelled. "Benjamin!" Caleb yelled. "We're over here!" Bell yelled. As I turned around I saw Bell laying on the floor next to Benjamin. "I found them!" I yelled.

Benjamin and Bell looked as if they were weak. As I ran toward them I saw Pandora sitting against the wall in the corner. She looked as if she was in a lot of pain. "Your going to be alright." I said as I knelt down beside Bell. "Benjamin, are you alright?" I asked. "Never better." Benjamin replied as he got up and picked up Bell off of the floor.

"Pandora?" Astarte said in a worried voice as he ran toward her. Pandora looked at him as if she was really shaken up. "What happened? Where's Ashley?" Shane asked as he knelt down to check on Pandora. "They took her." Pandora replied. "Eric and Melina broke into the temple a while ago. They took Ashley. They said that they want to finish what was started." Pandora added.

"Where are the children?" Raven asked looking worried. "I tried to stop them. They took the children with them." Pandora replied. "If anything happens to my daughter I will dedicate the rest of my immortal life to hunting them down and ripping their hearts out." Raven said as she began to look outraged.

"Nothing is going to happen to the children. I won't let it." I said. "Pandora, did Eric and Melina say where they were taking Ashley and the children?" I asked. "No, but they said that you would figure it out and when you did they would be waiting for you to come for them so that they could finish this once and for all." Pandora replied.

"Then I'll track them." I said as I started to walk toward the door. "Elizabeth, we need a plan first." Caleb said as he put his hand on my shoulder. "Then you better start planning. I'm going after Eric and Melina one way or the other." I replied. "Don't worry Pandora. I will get the children and Ashley back." I said as I put my hand on Pandora's shoulder.

"What do we do now?" Eve asked. "Rest. The sun will be coming up soon." I replied. "Your forgetting something." Mary said. "What's that?" I asked. "I have all of the potions now. There's enough for all of us to drink some. Once we do sunlight will no longer be an issue for us." Mary replied.

"Then lets drink." Caleb said. "I have over twenty potions in this bag. There's plenty for everyone." Mary replied. "When I give you a potion open it and drink all of it. The potion is made of Julian's blood. Be certain that you want this before you drink. The choice is yours." Mary added.

As Mary handed me a potion bottle I looked at Caleb. "Are you sure that this is what you want?" I asked. "Yes. I miss the sunlight Elizabeth. I want to be able to enjoy a simple human pleasure even if I'm not human anymore." Caleb replied. "Ok. Then I'm with you until the end."

As I opened the potion I felt a little happy. I guess I never really knew how much I missed the sunlight until this very moment. As I felt Julian's blood flow over my lips I felt as if there was something that was beginning to awaken in me.

Somehow I felt as if I had found the missing piece of the puzzle. I felt happy again. Happiness is hard to come by in a vampire's life. It's a feeling that we vampires rarely get to feel. I was happy to feel that once again but most importantly I was glad to be able to share that feeling with my family. The people that I cared the most about. As we all drank the potions that Mary gave us we each felt the rush of Julian's blood settle in on us like a burning fire.

There was no doubt that Julian was indeed an old vampire. His blood flowed through my veins like a burning fire and with each moment it spread like a wild fire through a forest. "The sun is rising." Caleb said.

"Lets go out and enjoy it." Bell said. As I walked outside of the temple with Bell and the others I felt like I had finally found a moment of peace. As the sun shined on all of us it felt warm. The light of the sun had no effect on us at all. I felt like I did with the sun when I was human.

Everyone was smiling. What we all thought was impossible turned out to be true. At last we were able to feel human again. As human as we could anyway. The simple pleasure of the sun was ours to enjoy once again. Now all there was to do was to get Ashley back from Eric and Melina. We had to take them out and do it now. Ashley's life depended on it.

Chapter 11

The Search

"I'm glad that we are all enjoying the sunlight but we need to find Ashley." I told them. "I agree." Shane said. "Where do we start?" Shane asked. "We start here and follow their scent to wherever they are." I replied. "How's that going to help?" Shane asked looking confused. "Eric and Melina said that I would figure out where they were. So obviously that means that all we have to do is follow their scent." I replied. "If they didn't want to tell us to follow their scent then they would have told Pandora where they were going." I added.

"That makes sense." Caleb said. "Let's get going then." Raven said. "Let's get our kids back." Raven said as she looked over at Pandora. "I'm with you." Pandora replied as she reached out and put her hand on Raven's shoulder. "What ever we do we have to stick together while we're tracking them. We can't split up." I told them. "Agreed." Astarte replied.

"If we split up we can cover more ground." Connor said. "Yes, but if we do that then we could fall under whatever traps that Eric and Melina have laid out for us." I replied. "With all of us hunting together its going to take longer to find Ashley." Rosemary said.

"Yes it will, but if we stick together we will have a better chance at taking on whatever Eric and Melina throw at us on the way." Astarte replied. "There's always been strength in numbers." Victor said. "Let's move out." I said. As we walked out of the temple and began to follow the trail of Eric and Melina's scent I knew that something wasn't right.

This was too easy. I knew that if Eric and Melina wouldn't tell Pandora where they were taking Ashley and the children that they must have had a good reason for doing so.

I was willing to bet anything that they had traps set out along their trail for us to fall into in order to delay us as much as possible. After all they seemed like the type that loved to play games.

In that moment I stopped as I looked around the woods trying to locate their scent. Their scent was all over the woods. In that moment I knew that they were trying to trick us by leading us around in circles so that we would never get to Ashley and the children in time to save them from whatever Eric and Melina had planned for them.

"What is it?" Eve asked. "Eric and Melina's scent is all over these woods." I replied. "Their trying to trick us into going around in circles aren't they?" Raven asked. "Yes." Shane replied. "So what do we do now?" Pandora asked. "We need to go where their scent is the strongest." I replied.

"Why do we need to do that?" Beth asked. "Because wherever their scent is the strongest is the way to follow them to wherever they have taken Ashley and the children." Amelia said. "You really are a good hunter." Phillip said in amazement. "Thank you." Amelia replied. "What can I say she's my wife." Darren said as he smiled at Amelia.

"Alright Elizabeth, lead us to them." Raven said. "We need to go north." I said as I started to walk again. "Then north is where we will go." Pandora said. As we walked north I started to feel like something was off.

I knew we were going the right way this time but I knew that something would be waiting gfor us ahead. "Your right." Amelia said. "About what?" I asked looking back at her confused. "I feel it too." Amelia replied.

"Feel what?" I asked looking confused again. "The strange feeling that Eric and Melina have laid out some sort of trap for us when we get to where they are." Amelia replied.

"I just know that this is way too easy." I said. "Yes it is." Caleb said as he walked up beside me. "Everyone stop! Bell sees something!" Benjamin yelled from back behind us. I stopped walking with the others and turned around to look at Bell. She looked as if she was troubled by something.

"What is it Bell?" I asked as I began to walk toward her. "They know that Ashley is with child." Bell replied. "How?" Shane asked looking worried as he put his hand on Bell's shoulder. "Melina used her power of glamour on Ashley in order to find out everything about us." Bell said as she opened her eyes.

"So what's the bad news.?" Mary asked. "Eric and Melina want to keep Ashley until she has the baby." Bell replied. "Why?" I asked. "They want if for theirselves." Bradley said as if he wasn't surprised by any of this. "Eric and Melina are just as blood thirsty and greedy for power as Julian was." Bradley added. "There not going to keep my child." Shane said.

"Your child?" Bradley asked as he looked as Shane with a confused look. "Yes dad. Ashley is carrying my child and I love her." Shane replied. Bradley looked over at Mary. "Why didn't you tell me that we were going to be grandparents?" Bradley asked.

"Small detail." Mary replied with a smile. "We were in the middle of trying to escape from Julian's castle. It just slipped my mind." Mary added. "Women." Bradley said shaking his head. "Hey I saved your but." Mary said as she looked over at Bradley with those golden bronze eyes as they began to widen by the minute. "Yes dear." Bradley replied as he kissed Mary on her cheek. "Marriage." Darren said shaking his head.

"What's wrong with marriage?" Amelia asked looking at Darren with wide eyes. "Nothing." Darren mumbled as he looked down at the ground. "Did you happen to see where Eric and Melina were?" I asked. "I saw some things around them but I'm not sure exactly where they are." Bell replied.

"What did you see?" Raven asked. "They were in a room with a fire place. Ashley was sitting in a chair but the children---." Bell stopped speaking and looked as if she was heart broken. "What about the children?" Raven asked looking worried. "The children are tied down to chairs with wooden stakes attached to cross bows in front of them." Bell said as she looked at Raven and Pandora with a worried face.

"That low life piece of scum!" Raven said outraged. "Calm down Raven. We will get our children back. I know it." Pandora said as she put her hand down on Raven's shoulder in order to calm her down.

"What else did you see?" Pandora asked. "It looked like they were in some sort of house. The room had a fire place and a wooden floor with a red carpet in the middle of the floor. It looked like they were in the living room of the house." Bell replied. "Why would they be in a house?" I asked looking curious.

"I don't know." Caleb replied. "Wait a minute. I think I know where Bell is talking about." Bradley said. "When I use to be Julian's servant I went with him to a cave that was located on a dessert. It was a cave that Julian had for him and his siblings that they could go to when they wanted to get away from the city." Bradley added.

"Then that's where they are." Bell said. "We need to keep moving. There's no time to lose." I told them. As we continued to walk north toward the dessert a bad feeling suddenly came over me. In the moment of that feeling I heard what sounded to be foot steps about a few yards away. "Everyone stop!" I yelled.

"What is it?" Alyssa asked. "There's something out there." I replied. We all stood there in the middle of the woods listening. I closed my eyes and started to smell the air. "Its not human, and its not a vampire either." I said as I opened my eyes. "Then what is it?" Mason asked. "Something unnatural." I replied. "Smells like an animal to me." Amelia said.

"Its an animal alright. A very unusual animal." I said as I looked around the woods. "Then it must be one of Eric's pet." Bradley said. "Pet?" I asked looking at Bradley with a confused look. "Yeah. Eric has a pet named Braxus. He's as tall as a human on all four legs if not taller." Bradley replied.

"So he's a dog?" Lex asked. "Yes, only he's not your average dog. He has three heads and he's mean as hell." Bradley replied. "Oh great. A mutt from hell." Alyssa said. "You could say that." Bradley replied. "So that rotten egg smell is Braxus then?" I asked. "Yes." Bradley replied with a smile. "Wonderful." I said in a sarcastic voice.

"So how do we kill him?" Mason asked. "The only way I can think of is to rip all three of his heads off." Mason added. "That's the only thing I can think of as well." Bradley replied. "Well that sounds all good and well but how are we going to do that when he's taller than us, not to mention that he has three heads one just as mean as the other?" Mary asked.

"We'll have to jump on his back and be able to hold on long enough to rip all of his heads off with our hands." I replied. "Sounds fun! I want to be one of the first to jump on him and rip a head off." Mason said in an excited voice. "Only Mason would say that." I said as I looked at the others.

"I'll rip the next one." Darren said. "So who gets the third?" Alyssa asked with a devilish smile on her face. "Oh no, don't even think about it." I said as I looked over at her. "What?" Alyssa said trying to look innocent. "I just wanted to have a little fun but I guess we can let the boys do it." Alyssa added. "I'll take the third." Lex said.

"I haven't had a chance to have fun any yet." Lex added with a smile on his face. "Alright. Lets draw the dog out." I said. "Like a moth to a flame." Mason said as he ran toward the woods behind Lex and Darren.

As the boys ran off I heard a growl. It sounded really close. "He's close!" Bradley yelled. In that moment I looked up to see Darren sitting in a tree next to Lex while Mason was in the tree across from them waiting for Braxus to come toward us so they could take him from behind. As I saw the birds fly from out of the trees I knew that Braxus was getting close.

In that moment I saw a huge black looking creature move toward me. "Its Braxus!" Bradley yelled. As I looked up I saw a four legged dog with black fur and yellow eyes looking down at me. The dog was much taller than me. He was taller than all of us. The dog looked as if he was nearly seven feet tall. As his eyes met with mine he growled.

As the dog opened his mouth to growl I could see his pearly white razor sharp teeth. His fangs looked to be about three inches long. He was the biggest creature that I had ever seen. His paws alone looked like they were as big as the feet on a giant. In the moment of that thought Braxus lifted one of his paws and smacked me across the woods causing me to hit a tree and roll down the hill.

"Elizabeth!" Alyssa yelled. Braxus turned toward Alyssa and smacked her across the ground. "Alyssa!" Mason yelled as he sat up in the tree waiting for Braxus to get closer. As Braxus stepped back in between the trees where Darren and the others were waiting I heard Astarte yell. "Now!"

As Mason and the others jumped on Braxus from behind trying to wrestle him down I was trying to make my way back up the hill to get to Alyssa. "They need help!" Raven yelled. "How?" Pandora asked. "It will take just about all of us but if we grab Braxus's paws we can pull him down to the ground and make it easier for the boys to rip him apart." Raven replied. "Alright." Pandora said. "Connor! Phillip!" Astarte called. "Help me pull one of Braxus's paws so we can get him down."

"I'll help." William said. "I'll help you." Victor said. "Caleb and I will take the back ones.." Amelia said. "Pandora and I can help." Raven replied. "I'll go tend to Alyssa." Star said. "I'll get Elizabeth." Rosemary replied. "I guess I'll just stand here with Eve and Athena and do nothing. "Beth said in a sarcastic voice as she crossed her arms.

"Everyone pull!" Astarte yelled. As they pulled Rosemary came down the hill to get me. "Elizabeth?" Rosemary said in a worried voice. "I'm alright." I replied. "Lets get back up there." Rosemary said. When Rosemary and I got back up the hill I saw Alyssa standing next to Star. "You almost have him!" Alyssa yelled. "Keep pulling!" Star yelled.

"This dog weighs a ton!" Victor yelled. "We've got to get him to the ground!" William yelled. "Pull!" Phillip yelled. "We are pulling!" Victor yelled in an irritated voice. While the others tried to pull Braxus down to the ground Darren, Lex, and Mason were having a hard trying to stay on Braxus's back to rip his heads off. "I can't catch any of his heads! He keeps moving them around!" Lex yelled. "Keep trying!" Darren yelled. In that moment Astarte and the others had pulled Braxus down to the ground.

"I got one!" Mason yelled. "Hold him down!" Darren yelled. "We're trying!" Astarte yelled. Mason wrapped his hands around one of Braxus's heads and ripped it off with no problem. As Mason ripped off one of the heads and threw it down on the ground Braxus began to scream. "Get the other ones!" Lex yelled. "We're trying!" Mason yelled.

"Hurry! We can't hold Braxus for long!" Astarte yelled. "They almost have him!" I yelled. Braxus was moving around so fast that the boys were having a hard time trying to catch the other heads.

After a moment Lex and Darren finally caught the other two heads and began to pull on them so they could rip them off from Braxus's body. "We got him!" Darren yelled. "Good! Now pull!" Alyssa yelled. As Darren and Lex pulled off the other two heads the dog growled and screamed in pain. As the last two heads fell to the ground Darren and the others jumped down off of Braxus and ran toward us. As the dog's body fell to the ground.

"Well that was fun." Darren said. "Yeah. It was a real work out." Mason replied. "I wonder what Eric and Melina have brewing up for us next." Lex said. "I don't know." I replied.

"All we can do now is keep moving and just take on whatever traps they have laid out for us." I added. "Whatever they have planned doesn't matter. We will get to Ashley and the children one way or the other." Raven said. "Come on. Let's keep moving." Caleb said.

As we continued to walk north I started to think about Ashley. I wondered what was all running through her mind. She must be scared out of her mind I thought. The worst part was wondering what Eric ad Melina were doing to her. I knew they wouldn't hurt her though. Not if they want her baby.

"They will keep her alive until the baby is born." Amelia said as she walked up beside me. "The baby will be born in a month." I replied. "Yes. It will take us that long to find her." Bell said as she walked behind me.

"Why that long?" I asked. "Because Eric and Melina have a long trail ahead of us and their location will take us that long to get to." Bell replied. "Why?" Alyssa asked. "Because their location is on the dessert and that is miles away from the city." Bell explained. "Now I understand." I said as I kept walking with the others. "Let the month begin." Darren said.

"At least we don't have to worry about the sunlight." I said as I looked over at Darren. As we kept walking I continued to think about Ashley. This was a long journey that laid ahead for us. We would all be walking for weeks to get to the dessert.

The hardest part was going to be doing this without rest. Our bodies were getting ready to be tested as well as our ability to deal with the sunlight. I knew that this would be a rough trip but getting to Ashley was important to me. I had to make it for her. Saving her life was worth much more to me than worrying about mine.

I didn't know what laid ahead for us when we got to the dessert but I knew that it was going to be a risk that we would all just have to take. Ashley's life as well as Sky's and Serenity's were on the line. Their lives not only depended on us but they rested in our hands.

All of our lives were at risk.

Chapter 12

Olivia

3 weeks had passed and we were getting closer to the dessert. I could tell that everyone was getting tired. We had walked non stop for 3 weeks now. The only time that we stopped was to hunt. I decided to stop and let everyone rest and hunt beings we were only a day away from the dessert now. I knew that all of us would have to be at our best if we were going to take on Eric and Melina. "Lets camp here by the river." I said. "We can hunt in the woods and then we can rest for a while." I added.

"Sounds good to me." Victor replied. "I hear a panther." Amelia said. "Anyone care to join me?" Amelia asked. "Right behind you." Darren replied. "There's a couple of deers as well." Caleb said. "Lets go catch them." Mason replied. "Are you coming?" Alyssa asked as she looked over toward me.

"You all go ahead. I'll catch up with you in a minute." I replied. As Alyssa and the others went to hunt I started gathering up some fire wood. As I gathered up some wood I heard a rabbit near by. I put the fire wood down slowly and began to move in on the rabbit.

It was behind the bushes. I could hear the rabbit's heart beat faster as I got closer to the bushes. I knelt down and reached out to grab the rabbit. As I held the rabbit in my hand I began to feed on it.

As I felt the rabbit's blood go down my throat I began to feel better. I felt as if I had all my strength back again. I felt like I was back to my old self. After I was done eating I picked up the fire wood and headed back to the camp site by the river.

When I got to the camp site I saw a tall woman with a long curly black hair and red eyes looking at me as if she had been waiting for me. She had on a long black dress with a red corset over it. She looked like a witch. She was rather frightening to look at. "Who are you?" I asked as I put the fire wood on the ground.

"Are you Elizabeth?" The woman asked. "Yes." I replied. "Now who are you?" I asked once again. "I am Olivia." The woman replied. "What are you doing here?" I asked. "I am here to help you defeat Eric and Melina." Olivia replied. "Well done on defeating Julian." Olivia added.

"How much do you know about that?" I asked. "Because she's Julian's witch." Mary said as she walked up behind me with the others. "Yes. I was his servant but not anymore." Olivia replied. "Why have you come?" Mary asked. "She wants to help us take on Eric and Melina." I replied. "Very good." Olivia said. "We don't need your help Olivia." Mary said. "If you want to defeat Eric and Melina you will need all of the help that you can get. I can give you that." Olivia replied.

"What's in it for you?" Mary asked. "Your more clever than I thought Mary." Olivia said as she began to smile. "Comes with the territory." Mary replied with a slight grin. "Very well. In return for helping you defeat Eric and Melina I want you to help me become the rightful ruler of Egypt." Olivia said.

"And why would I do that?" Mary asked. "Simple. You want to be human again. I can make that happen." Olivia replied. "You can turn us all back into humans?" I asked. "Yes."

"She's full of it." Bradley said. "Am I?" Olivia said as she smiled once again. "How do I know that your telling the truth?" Mary asked. "You don't, but if you want to defeat Eric and Melina as well as get Ashley and the children back I'd say that you would just have to trust me." Olivia replied. "How can we trust her?" I asked. "You don't have a choice."

"As much as I hate to admit it Olivia's right." Mary said. "You can't be serious!" Bradley said outraged. "You mean your going to trust her?" Shane asked. "Yes. It's the only chance we have." Mary replied. "This is insane." Shane said. "I don't trust Olivia either, but Pandora and I want our children back." Raven said as she put her hand on Shane's shoulder.

"Know this Olivia, if you are leading us into a trap and something happens to my child or Pandora's child I will kill you." Raven as she looked over at Olivia. "My don't you have a fire about you." Olivia replied. "More than you know." Raven said with a smile. "Mother's are always protective of their young." Pandora said. "I see that." Olivia replied.

"Alright Olivia, we will let you help us." I told her. "Good decision." Olivia replied. "We will camp here tonight. We will leave for the dessert in the morning." Astarte said. "Fine with me." Olivia replied. "I'm in need of some blood. I think I'll go hunting. Catch you all later." Olivia said as she walked away.

After Olivia left I began to start a fire. As I sat around the fire with the others through out the night while Olivia was out on her hunting spree I started to think about Ashley again. Before I knew it Caleb began to speak interrupting my thoughts.

"I don't trust her. Olivia knows more that she's letting on." Caleb said. "She wants us to kill Eric and Melina so she can claim the throne and become the ruler of Egypt." Bell said as she walked up behind us. "That much is obvious." Amelia replied. "Olivia also plans on having us killed after she becomes queen." Bell said. "I knew it!" Darren said.

"That witch is playing us like pieces on a game board." Darren added. "No she's not." I said. "How do you figure that?" Victor asked. "Because while Olivia thinks that she has us right where she wants us we know different." I replied. "What do you mean?" Darren asked.

"She means that Olivia only offered to turn us into humans because she knew that we wouldn't refuse that offer if it were truly possible." Amelia replied. "Olivia made us the only offer that she knew would get our attention." Amelia added. "Olivia has the power to see another person's weakness. That's how she knew what to offer us." Mary said.

"Well that explains her interest in wanting our help." Alyssa said. "So what do we do in the mean time?" Mason asked. "We play along." Star replied. "That's right. As long as we play Olivia's little game we will be ok." I told them. "Once we defeat Eric and Melina we take Olivia out." I added. "Good plan." Alyssa said with a slight smile on her face. "Your sister is quite diabolical Alyssa." Lex said.

"What can I say? She's my sister." Alyssa replied. "Your just as bad as Elizabeth is." Mason said as he put his arm around Alyssa and kissed her on the lips. "Yep and you love it." Alyssa replied with a grin. "Yeah I do." Mason said as he leaned in to kiss Alyssa once again. "Alright you two. That's enough." I told them. "Lets get some rest. We have a long day ahead of us tomorrow." I added.

As I slept I began to dream of Ashley. It was as if she had came to me of her own free will. "Elizabeth?" Ashley said in a low voice. "Ashley?" I said as I began to walk toward her. "I don't have a lot of time to explain. I'm using all of the energy that I have left to speak to you." Ashley said as she walked toward me.

"Energy? What are you talking about?" I asked looking confused. "I'm a witch. I've never told anybody that. Not even Mason. No one is to know that yet. Olivia is working with Eric and Melina. She's leading all of you into a trap." Ashley replied. "I know. I've known that since she first arrived."

"Eric promised Olivia that if she kills you and your family that she will sit at his side as his queen of Egypt." Ashley continued. "Well that makes a lot more since then." I replied. "You must kill Olivia. You have to kill her now. If you don't you and your family will be in danger." Ashley warned me.

"How do I kill a witch?" I asked. "I know that she's a vampire but she's part witch too." I added. "There's only one thing that can kill a witch who is undead. You must go to the temple of Zan. It's a place of ultimate power. It holds the only object in the world that can kill a witch who is undead." Ashley replied. "What is it?" I asked. "It's a dagger." Ashley replied.

"A dagger? You mean to tell me that I have to go all the way to some temple for a dagger?" I asked in an annoyed voice. "Yes. This is not just any dagger. It's the dagger of Zan. Its very powerful and it has the power to kill any witch who is undead. Meaning any witch who has been made a vampire." I looked at Ashley annoyed.

"You wait until I'm a day away from the dessert as well as so close to rescuing you and the children to tell me this!" I said in an irritated voice. "I know your irritated with me, but first thing is first. You have to kill Olivia. If you don't you will regret it." Ashley replied. "Kill Olivia and then come to the dessert and get me and the children." Ashley added.

"What are you going to do in the mean time?" I asked. "Eric and Melina have no idea that I'm a witch. They are not aware of the power that I carry. I can protect the children and amuse Eric until you and the others get here." I have to say I was impressed with Ashley's quick thinking. "Raven and Pandora will never go for this. They want their kids." I replied.

"Shane is already upset enough as it is. If I ask him to wait about you he will hit the roof." I added. "Then let me speak through you." Ashley replied. "You can do that?" I asked in disbelief. "Yes. I can do a lot of things." I couldn't help but to be amazed.

"Ok, but when all of this is over you have to tell me how you became a witch and about your powers." I replied. "Interested are we?" Ashley teased. "Very." I said with a slight grin. "I will only be able to speak to the others through you for a few minutes. I'm starting to feel weak."

"Alright. I'll wake up and tell the others what's going on. After I do that you come into my body and explain the rest." I said as I began to walk away. "Agreed." As I woke up I saw the others laying around on the ground sleeping. Olivia was still gone. She was still hunting. I knew I had to wake the others up and tell them what was going on before Olivia got back.

"Everyone wake up!" I yelled. As the others woke up they looked at me worried. "What's wrong?" Star asked. "Elizabeth has had a vision." Bell replied. "An interesting vision." Amelia said. "What is it?" Shane asked. "I saw Ashley. She came to me." I replied. "What?" Victor said in disbelief.

"How could a human come to you?" William asked. "Ashley's not just a human." I replied. "Then what is she?" Benjamin asked. "I can't explain that now. Ashley is going to come and speak through me. I want all of you to listen to her. Especially you Shane. Its important." I told them.

"Alright." Shane replied. "Ashley you can come to me now. I invite you in." I said as I closed my eyes. In a matter of seconds I began to feel something reach inside me. It was like something was pushing its way inside of my body. After a moment I opened my eyes. "Ashley?" Shane said.

"Yes. I don't have much time. I can only speak through Elizabeth for a moment." Everyone looked as if they were amazed. "What's going on and how are you able to enter Elizabeth's body?" Shane asked.

"I'm a witch. I can't explain all of that now but you must listen to what I am about to tell you. You all are in danger. You must kill Olivia. She has no intention of helping you except to your deaths. She's working with Eric and Melina."

"Are the children alright?" Raven asked. "Yes. I can protect them until you all arrive to help us. I told Elizabeth about the temple of Zan, you must go there and get the dagger of Zan in order to kill Olivia. It's the only weapon in the world that can kill a witch who has been made a vampire."

Everyone stood there in silence for a moment. "We will do that." Pandora said. "Eric and Melina have no idea that I'm a witch. I can amuse Eric long enough for you all to get the dagger and come to the dessert. Melina however is going to be hard to amuse."

"We will get the dagger Ashley and we will save you and the children from those low lives." Astarte said. "I must go now. I can't stay in Elizabeth's body for long. I'm starting to get weak. It took all of the energy that I had to get this message to all of you. I must rest and regain my strength." In that moment I felt Ashley's hold on me begin to release. "Elizabeth?" Caleb said.

"Yeah. Its me. Ashley's gone. We need to get started. We need to take out Olivia and get to Ashley and the children before its too late." I replied. "Mary, do you know where the temple of Zan is?" I asked. "Yes. I can lead you to it. It's about two days away from here." Mary replied. "Two days! We don't have time to fool around! Ashley is in danger!" Shane said in an irritated voice.

"So are the children!" Raven yelled. "Alright!" I yelled as I stepped in between them. "Lead me to the temple Mary." I said. "Your not going alone." Caleb said. "Yes I am. I need you to go with the others in case something happens. Mary and I will be fine." I replied. "What about the rest of us?" Eve asked.

"Olivia will lead the rest of you to the dessert. She wants to lead you to Eric and Melina so they can kill all of you on sight. When you get to the dessert do what you can against Eric and Melina and get Ashley and the children out of there.

When Mary and I get back we will kill Olivia and then I will deal with Eric and Melina." I replied. "No. I will deal with Melina." Mary said. "Why you?" I asked. "Because Melina killed your father. She is responsible for everything that has happened." Mary replied.

I was speechless. There were no words to describe my feelings at that moment. I had no idea what to say much less what to feel. I felt sorry for Mary but I couldn't feel much of anything else. Truth be told I never knew the man that Mary spoke off. The only love of a father I had ever known had been dead for years now.

"Alright. When we get to the dessert you can take on Melina." I told her. "You two better get going. You have a long journey ahead of you.

"I will." I said as I leaned over to kiss Caleb on his soft lips. "Mason, take good care of my sister." I said as I walked over to hug him. "You know I will." Mason replied as he wrapped his arms around me. "Come back in one piece." Alyssa teased as she wrapped her arms around me. "Don't worry. I'll make it back. Nothing could ever keep me away from you." I replied. "Well at least you and Mary will get to talk on the way." Alyssa said as she looked at me and smiled.

"Oh yeah. I just can't wait for that." I said in a sarcastic voice. "Be nice." Caleb said as he kissed my cheek. "I'll see you soon." I replied as I kissed Caleb one last time. "You better." Caleb said. I walked over toward Mary as her and Bradley were saying their goodbyes. "Be safe my love." Bradley said. "Always." Mary replied as she put her hand on Bradley's cheek as she leaned in to kiss him.

"Come on Mary. We need to get going." I told her. As Mary and I started walking off into the woods I began to wonder if this was part of my destiny. It was obvious that I was meant to become a vampire and experience things that only mortals could dream about.

I felt as if Mary and I would become close on this journey like Shane and I had with in a few nights. I guess no matter how much I tried to resent Mary she would always be my mother whether I liked it or not.

As true as that may be though, Mary would never be able to replace the mother that I had for all of my life that I recently lost in such a short time after my birth into darkness as I call it. Mary may be the one who gave me life but the mother I had gave me love as well as a life that I would give up eternity just to have again.

It didn't matter what happened on this journey between Mary and I. My mind was set on the challenge ahead. Getting the dagger. Having a family reunion was the least of my concern. Ashley and the children were the only concern that I had now.

For I would save them and go on about my immortal life as I had before. In the end Mary was going to be just another soul of the damned that I had came across in my eternal life in the darkness. What happened between us after this mission was of as little importance to me.

I didn't care to know Mary. The only thing that I cared about was saving the ones that I did care about. Ashley, Sky, and Serenity. Nothing else mattered. To me this was just business. Just another mission to accomplish. Nothing that Mary would say on our journey would make me feel any sort of compassion for her. Or so I thought.

Chapter 13

Revealing The Past

As Mary and I walked on our journey to the temple of Zan Mary began to speak of my father. Will Meadows. I tried to act as if I wasn't interested but it seemed as if Mary knew me all to well. It was as if she could see right through me. Why not just listen to what she has to say? After all, I might as well make the best of this trip. Might as well be as entertained as possible.

"You know your father was a great fisherman. We use to go out on his boat in the ocean and catch enough seafood to eat for months." Mary said trying to start a conversation. "Did you ever like seafood?" Mary asked. "Yeah. I liked shrimp." I replied. "Me too." Mary said with a slight smile.

"Would you like to know how I met your father?" Mary asked. "Why not. We might as well make some sort of conversation on the way." I replied. "I get the feeling that you don't like me very much." Mary said as she began to look as if she was sad.

"That's not true." I said as I looked over at her with a slight smile on my face. "It isn't?" Mary asked looking surprised. "No." I replied. "I don't like you at all." I said as I looked at her with an angry face. "I'm sorry you feel that way." Mary said in a low voice.

"I'm sure the sight of me makes you sick. You must feel a lot of anger toward me." Mary added. "How I feel about you doesn't matter. When all of this is over we will never see each other again." I replied. "You hate me that much huh?" Mary asked. "I hate you for coming into my life the way that you have!" I said in an angry voice. "You could of done what you always have and just stayed out of my life!" I yelled.

"Look, I made some mistakes and I hurt you. I'm sorry for that, but if you never remember anything from our time together than remember this, even though I gave you up for my own selfish reasons, not a day has gone by that I didn't think about you." Mary said. "Why did you give me up? I mean what was the real reason?" I asked in a frustrated voice.

"I was afraid." Mary replied. I stopped walking and looked at her with an even more furious expression. "Afraid?" I said in disbelief. "Afraid of what?" I asked as I started to become more furious.

"I was afraid of raising you all alone." Mary replied. "That's it?" I asked in a frustrated voice once again. "Yeah." Mary said as she looked as if she was ashamed of something. "Call me crazy, but I don't think that your telling the truth." I said as I started to walk again. "Your right. I'm not." Mary replied.

"So what is the truth then?" I asked. I was beginning to feel even more and more frustrated. "When your father was murdered by Melina I started to feel afraid for you. I thought that she would come after you next. Because of that I decided to give you to someone who ii thought would take good care of you."

In some strange way I began to understand why Mary did what she did. This reason made a lot more since to me than the first. I didn't feel as angry anymore. I felt kind of grateful. "Well I guess I can understand that." I replied.

"I guess I shouldn't be angry at you. In a way I should be grateful to you for what you did." I added. "Grateful? Why do you say that?" Mary asked looking confused. "Because if it wasn't for you I wouldn't had the chance to experience what having a good mother was like."

"I understand. I know that I can never replace Lisa. She was a good woman." In that moment I started to think about my mother. "Yes she was." I replied. "Lets just forget about the past and start over." I said. "I'd like that."

I guess Mary wasn't so bad after all. I guess getting to know her wouldn't be so bad. Whether I liked it or not Mary was my real mother. Getting to know her couldn't hurt. I mean we were on a two day journey. Why not make conversation?

"Would you like to hear about your father?" Mary asked. "Sure." I replied. "Your father was a good man. He was a great fisherman." Mary started in. "Have you ever been to the Pensacola Beach?" Mary asked. "Yeah. I used to go there with my dad and pick sea shells." I replied.

Mary smiled as she started to speak again.

"It was a hot summer day. I was swimming with some friends down at the beach when I first saw your father. He was standing out on the peer with some of his friends watching me."

"I bet I know what happened next." I said with as I looked over at Mary and smiled. "You have your father's sense of humor." Mary replied as she smiled back at me. "I remember what I thought the first time that I looked at your father." Now I knew where this was going. "What were your thoughts?" I asked trying to take an interest.

"Your father was the most handsome man that I had ever seen. He was beautiful. Dark hair and dark eyes." Mary replied. "And now you have Bradley." I said interrupting Mary from her thoughts.

"Yes. Bradley is a good man. He saved me from my depression. I was at the end of my rope before I met Bradley. When Melina killed your father I was put into a state of grief that I had never been in before."

"Caleb said that Will was mugged in an alley." I said looking confused. "That's what I told Caleb. He and the others didn't know the truth until I mentioned it before we left." Mary replied.

"I see. Losing Will must have been very hard for you." In that moment a tear of blood rolled down Mary's face. "It was. I felt as if I lost the other half of my soul. Well, when I had a soul." Mary smiled as she said those last words.

"Don't get me wrong. I love Bradley, but even he knows the love that I had for your father was real. It was unconditional. I may love Bradley, but I will always love your father as well."

"Melina must have caused you a lot of pain. I could only imagine how I would be if I were to lose Caleb." Saying those last words made me feel sorry for Mary. She had lost a lot. I could only imagine what she had went through.

"Can I ask you something?" I asked. "Of course." Mary replied. "Why did Melina kill Will?" Mary looked as if she didn't want to answer that question. "Elizabeth, there is more to this than you know. There is something about your father that you don't know."

I looked at Mary with a worried look. I wasn't sure if I wanted to her to answer my question. "Your father was a very gifted man. At one time he was a servant of Melina's and her family." Mary replied.

"Your father had a gift for being able to see the future through dreams." Mary added.

"Kind of like what I have?" I asked interrupting her. "Yes. Your father was able to see things in his dreams like you can. I guess he passed that gift on to you." Mary took a deep breath and started to speak again. "One day your father grew tired of Melina and her family. He was tired of being a servant of pure evil."

"Why did he ever start serving Melina?" I asked. "About a year before I met your father, Melina and her family were out hunting one night. They came across your father and his family in the woods. Your father and your grandfather liked to go hunting. Your aunt and your grandmother went with them that evening. They waited by the camp fire for your father and your grandfather to return. I guess you could say that your grandmother and your aunt weren't much for hunting." Mary began to look as if she was heart broken. After a moment she started to speak again.

"While your father and your grandfather were out hunting, Melina and her family came across your aunt and your grandmother. They killed them. When your father and your grandfather returned they saw nothing but blood on the ground. As they looked up into the trees they saw your aunt and your grandmother hanging by their necks with their insides ripped out of them. Melina and her family came out from behind the trees and attacked your grandfather while they made your father watch. Melina sensed something in your father that she felt was special. Melina took your father back to her family's castle and made your father her servant. She thought that having your father around would be useful to her because of his gift."

In that moment I felt as if I was heart broken. I began to feel even more sorry for Mary. She had obviously been through more than I had realized. "I'm sorry to hear that." I said. "What else happened?" I asked.

"The following year I met your father. After your father met me he decided that he wanted to leave Melina and her family in order to be with me. Melina of course was furious. She loved your father. Melina had planned to turn your father and have him as her companion for eternity but as you know that didn't happen." Mary replied.

"So that's why Melina killed him? Because he loved you and not her?" I asked. "Yes. In a way your father's death is my fault." Now I understood everything. Everything that I have been through was all because of Melina. If it wasn't for her I would have had the chance to know my real parents.

I would have been able to stay human and therefore I would have never been turned into the creature that I've been for years now. In the moment of that thought I began to feel a rage come over me. I began to feel hatred toward Melina. Yes. This was all Melina's fault. She is responsible for all of this! "I can feel your rage." Mary said. "I guess its all starting to settle in." I replied.

Then again, maybe I should be grateful to Melina. If she hadn't of killed my real father and by doing so had forced Mary to give me up then I wouldn't have ever known Lisa. The mother I had for all of these years that I loved so much. I wouldn't have ever known what having a sister like Alyssa was like or even met Caleb for that matter.

Caleb was my true love. There was no doubt about that. Yes, if it wasn't for Melina I would have never met any of these people that I loved so much. Thank you Melina, I thought. Thank you for giving me the good life that I had. However, you are my enemy for you did kill my real father, and for that you must die. In that moment Mary spoke again interrupting me from my thoughts.

"Now you understand why I have to kill Melina." Mary said. "Yes I do. The sooner we get to the temple of Zan the quicker we will be able to get back to the others and save Ashley and the children as well as take out Melina forever." I replied. "Are you with me?" I asked. "Lets do this." Mary replied.

I guess the two of us working together wasn't as bad as I thought. Who knows, maybe after all of this is done we can get to know each other better. Maybe Mary will stick around for a while along with Shane and Bradley so I can get to know all of them better. Temple of Zan here I come.

Chapter 14

The Temple Of Zan

It had been two days now since Mary and I left the others and began our journey to the temple of Zan. I knew that it was only a matter of time before Olivia led the others into the trap that she had set for them. I knew that Mary and I had to hurry and get back to the others soon for Eric and Melina would kill them all. As Mary and I walked up the steps of the temple I began to feel dizzy once again. Not now I thought. This is not the time for me to be getting dizzy.

As we walked up the steps I began to stumble. "What's wrong?" Mary asked. "I'm feeling dizzy again." I replied. Mary looked as if she knew what was going on. Come to think of it ever since I started my dizzy spells everyone has been acting strange. "Your going to be alright. Just take it easy." Mary told me. I nodded and began to walk up the steps once again. Mary stayed close to my side in case I started to stumble again.

As we walked up the steps I saw two guards standing in front of the entrance to the temple. They were human. Well that's new, I thought. "Let me do the talking." Mary said. "Halt." One of the guards said. "What is your purpose here?" The guard asked.

"We are here to see the legendary dagger of Zan." Mary replied.

"This is my daughter Elizabeth and I am Mary. We are tourists from America." Mary added. "Well sorry to disappoint you, but showing of the dagger has been over with for an hour now. We will be showing it again in the morning." The other guard said. "Couldn't you make an acception? I mean we came all this way----."

"I'm sorry, but we can not let you in until the morning." The guard said interrupting Mary. "Well, then I guess we're just going to have to kill you." Mary said with a slight smile. The guards began to laugh. Mary and I looked at each other and smiled.

After a moment we grabbed the guards by their throats and lifted them up in the air as we began to choke the life out of them. "Why don't we just eat them?" I asked as I smiled at Mary with a devilish grin. "Well normally I'd say you had a point, but I'm not really hungry." Mary replied. "Oh well. Suit yourself, but I'm eating mine." I said as I began to sink my teeth into the guard's throat.

As I fed Mary threw the other guard down on the ground. He was dead. Mary had choked the life out of him. After I finished feeding on the other guard I threw him down on the ground as well. "I guess we really are monsters." I said as I wiped the blood off of my lips. "We are what we are." Mary replied.

"I still don't see why we have to kill innocent people. Maybe after this I will only kill murderers or thieves or something." I said as I finished wiping the blood off of my lips. "That's a good idea." Mary said as she opened the doors to the temple. "Lets get that dagger." Mary added.

"Where is it?" I asked. "I don't know. Lets look around." Mary replied. As Mary began to walk around the room to try and find the dagger I decided to walk down the hall. The walls were made out of golden stones. At the end of the hall were two golden doors.

"What are you doing?" Mary asked as she walked up behind me. "I think the dagger may be in here." I replied as I opened the doors. As we walked inside the room I saw the dagger setting on a glass table with four silver legs underneath it made out of marble.

"There it is." Mary said as I began to walk toward the table. As I picked up the dagger I couldn't help but to look at it in amazement.

It was so beautiful. The blade shined as the sun began to reflect off of it.

It was as shiny as a crystal. The handle looked as if it was made out of white marble. As the sun hit the marble on the dagger it shined like it was filled with tiny little crystals. On the center of the handle was a green emerald. It was the most beautiful weapon that I had ever seen. For a double edged knife anyway.

"So this is the dagger of Zan." I said as I stood there by the table holding the dagger in my hand. "Yep, and now that we have it we need to get back to the others." Mary replied. "Yeah. Lets go." I said as I turned around and walked toward the doors. "Is it just me or was this way too easy?" Mary asked as we walked down the hall.

"It was too easy." I replied as we walked out of the temple. "I wonder if there was a catch to it." Mary said. As we walked back toward the direction of the dessert I thought about Mary's words. They made a lot of since. There had to be a catch. This was way too easy. However, the temple was guarded by humans. Maybe it was nothing. Maybe we shouldn't be worried at all.

"The temple was guarded by humans so maybe this was just too easy." I said as we kept walking. "Your probably right." Mary replied. "We need to move quickly. The others should be at the dessert by now. Olivia won't hesitate to try and kill them once she has them in Eric and Melina's grasp." Mary added.

"I agree. Lets run like the wind." In that moment Mary and I began to run through the woods. We flew passed the trees like a hurricane. There was no time to lose. We had to get to the others fast. All of their lives depended on us.

Mary and I ran through the woods until the sun went down. It was at that moment when we heard a noise in the woods. It sounded like a hissing noise. It wasn't an animal or a human. It wasn't even another vampire. Whatever it was it smelled like fowl. "What is that noise?" I asked.

"I don't know, but I don't like it." Mary said as she looked around the woods. "I'm starting to feel like we shouldn't have taken that dagger." Mary added. Mary and I kept looking around the woods. We didn't see anything out of the ordinary. In that moment we heard the hissing noise once again.

"There it is again." I said as I kept looking around the woods. "Yeah. I have a feeling that we're about to find out what it is. The noise is coming from the trees." Mary said as she glanced up at the trees. As I looked up I could see something moving through the trees, but I couldn't figure out what it was.

It was moving so fast that my eyes couldn't even catch a glimpse of what it was. Not even a human could see it. "Elizabeth, keep that dagger out. Your going to need it." Mary said. "Come out, come out, whatever you are!" Mary yelled.

After a moment I heard the hissing noise again. As I looked up at the trees I saw the fowl smelling creature drop to the ground. As it rose up I began to see what it was. The creature had a tongue like a slithering serpant and eyes as red as human blood. It had sparkling white fangs about two inches long.

The creature's whole body was black as night and looked to be about 30 feet long. It was a snake obviously. I knew that Mary and I were about to be in some serious trouble as the creature kept looking us over with its eyes.

The snake had the look of a predator in its eyes. It kind of reminded me of the look in a vampire's eyes before they made their kill. It was a look that I was familiar with. The look of a blood thirsty tyrant before coming in for the kill. Now I knew what it was like to be the prey.

"Get that dagger ready." Mary whispered. "Don't worry. I've got it ready to go." I replied. "Who are your creature and what do you want?" I asked. The creature stayed silent and looked at me as if it was amazed by something.

"I don't think it's in the mood to talk." Mary said as she kept looking at the creature. "Well it's here for some reason." I replied. "I'm guessing its because of the dagger." I added with a smile on my face. In that moment the creature hissed as if it was angry.

"Yep. I think that's it." I said smiled once again. "I told you this was too easy!" Mary yelled. "Nothing is ever easy for a vampire Mary. We're always in some kind of trouble at some point or another."

The creature began to move toward us. I was ready for a fight. I could sense that the creature had came for one. It may have been some sort of protector for the dagger but that didn't matter to me. I needed this dagger in order to save my friends. There was no way that I was about to give up this dagger with out a fight.

In the moment of that thought the creature began to open its mouth to speak. I wondered what the creature was about to say. My luck it would probably say that it was the protector of the dagger and that we were going to die for stealing it.

Let the creature try to take it from me. It will have no head before I'm done with it. Nothing was going to stop me from saving my friends. Nothing.

Chapter 15

Cyrus

I stood there waiting for the creature to speak. After a moment it did. "I am Cyrus. I am the keeper of the dagger that you have taken." Yep. There it was. It was just like I thought. The creature was here for the dagger. Looks like I'm going to have to fight the creature after all. "We don't want any trouble, but I need this dagger to save my friends." I told the creature. "I'm afraid I can't allow you to carry out your mission. The dagger belongs to the temple of Zan. I want it back now." The creature replied.

"What happens if I refuse to give up the dagger?" I asked with a slight smile. The creature looked as if it was annoyed. "If you refuse to give me the dagger then you and your friend will die." As the creature spoke those last words I looked over at Mary. "Are you ready for a fight?" I asked.

"Do we have a choice?" Mary said as she looked at me and smiled. "Sorry Cyrus, but I need the dagger to carry out my mission. I guess we're just going to have to fight for it." I said as I smiled once again.

In that moment Cyrus began to laugh. "You defeat me? Not likely." Cyrus said laughing. "I figured you would say something like that." I replied. "Give me the dagger!" Cyrus hissed. "Sorry. Its not for sale."

I replied. "Then I will take it from you!" Cyrus hissed in an angry voice.

"Come and get some." I replied as I grabbed Mary by the arm and began to run through the woods. "Elizabeth!" Mary yelled as we ran through the woods. "Elizabeth, why are we running when we could be fighting Cyrus?" Mary asked as we kept running.

"I'm forcing Cyrus into a trap." I replied. "Trap? What trap?" Mary asked. "I'm going to count to three. When I say three we will run off in different directions." I replied as I kept running. "How is that going to help? Mary asked looking confused. "You'll see." Cyrus was catching up to us and was just as fast as we were.

"Ready?" I asked. "As ready as I'll ever be." Mary replied. "One, two, three!" I yelled. In that moment Mary and I split up. I ran to the right while she ran to the left. Cyrus continued to run after me. I ran toward a mess of trees and jumped through them. As I did Cyrus jumped through the trees and got tangled up in them without realizing it.

I started to run toward Mary as Cyrus began to follow. Cyrus tried to get out of the trees to come after us. Cyrus's body was tied up around the trees. "Stop!" I yelled at Mary. Mary and I flashed over to where Cyrus was. "Looks like your in quite a tangle there." I said teasing Cyrus.

"I will get loose and when I do I will enjoy ripping you both apart piece by piece." Cyrus replied. "You won't live that long." I said as I took out the dagger and stabbed Cyrus in the throat.

"So much for ripping us up in pieces now." I said as I jumped up on top of Cyrus's head and began to cut it off. After I cut off

Cyrus's head I jumped down next to Mary. "Lets get to the dessert." I told her as I wiped off the dagger and put it in my pocket. "Good job kid." Mary replied. "Thanks."

"I hope we can reach others in time. Its going to take us a few days to get back to the camp site. The dessert is a day away from there after that." I added. "We'll have to run or fly." Mary replied. "Its getting dark now. We can fly without being spotted by the humans if we keep to the trees." I said.

"Good idea. Lets go." Mary said as she began to levitate up into the air. "Right behind you." I said as I started to fly up into the air. We flew all night and kept to the trees so that the humans wouldn't spot us.

When the sun started to come up the next day we ran through the woods until night came again. It would only be one more day now until we reached the dessert. I just hoped that we would make it in time to save the others. I prayed that we weren't too late. For if we were I would never forgive myself.

Chapter 16

The Dessert

Mary and I had traveled for days now without stopping to rest of hunt. We were about to enter the dessert when I began to feel dizzy again. "Wow!" I said as I stumbled over toward Mary. "Are you ok?" Mary asked looking worried. "Yeah. I just got dizzy again. When this is all over I'm going to find someone that I can go to in order to find out what's wrong with me." I replied. "Maybe we should stop and rest." Mary said as she held my arm.

"I can't. I have to get to the others." I said as I began to walk again. "We're almost there. We're about to enter the dessert. The cave isn't that far. We should be getting there soon." Mary replied. "Do you have a plan?" Mary asked. "No. We go in there and do the best that we can." I replied.

"Sounds wonderful." Mary said in a sarcastic voice. "Do you have an idea?" I asked. "No." Mary replied. "Then lets just do the best that we can." As Mary and I walked into the dessert toward the cave I wondered what would be waiting for us when we got there.

I wondered if Olivia had betrayed the others already and led them to their deaths. If anything happened to my family I would spend the rest of eternity making her pay. After walking about thirty miles in the dessert I saw the cave. It looked like a dark lair of some sort.

Like a cursed place in a dark realm or something. "This is it." I said as I looked over at Mary and began to walk toward the entrance of the cave. "Elizabeth wait." Mary said as she grabbed my arm. "What is it?" I asked.

"If something happens and I don't make it out I want you to know something." I looked at Mary a little worried. I wasn't sure of what she was about to say. "I may have made a terrible mistake by giving you up, but I just wanted you to have a good life without having to worry about people coming for you because of your father and I." In that moment I felt a tear of blood fall down my face as I looked at Mary.

"I was angry before, but now I understand why you did what you did. I may have never got to know you and Will, but because of the two of you I got the chance to know two good people. I got to know what having good parents were like." I said as I wiped the tears of blood off of my face.

"When this is all over you and I can get to know each other." I added. "I would like that." Mary replied. "Lets give these vampire scums a fight that they will never forget." I said as I reached out to grasp Mary's hand. As Mary and I entered the cave it was cold and dark.

Mary and I could see our way in the dark though. That was another good thing about being a vampire. Our vision was never limited. We could find our way around in the dark a lot better than a human could.

"They're close. I can smell them." I said. As Mary and I kept walking down the cave I started to see light coming down from the end. As I came closer I saw that it was fire. There were lit torches down through the cave. "We're getting close." Mary said. As we kept walking I could smell Olivia along with Eric and Melina. The scent of the others followed. After a while Mary and I entered the room. Now there was something bizarre. A room in a cave. Things were definitely getting strange. The room had a grey stone floor. There was a fire place to the left side of the room along with the pictures on the walls.

The walls were made of stone as well. They were just as grey as the floor. There was a wooden chair next to the fire place. As Mary and I walked through the room the scent of Olivia and the others became stronger.

As I looked over to the right of the room I saw a hall way. It looked as if it led to another room. The hallway was made of black stones. "The scent is stronger that way." I said as I pointed down the hall and began to walk toward the other room. There were torches lit along the hallway as well. As I got closer to the room the scent became even stronger.

As I entered the room I saw the others hanging from the wall wrapped in golden chains. Caleb was wrapped up with Alyssa and Mason. Amelia, Star, Victor, and Darren were wrapped up next to Lex and his family. Astarte was wrapped up with Pandora while Connor and Rosemary were wrapped up with Beth and Phillip.

Raven was wrapped up with Bell and Benhamin while Bradley and Shane were wrapped up next to them. Sky and Serenity were tied up and hanging above a stone table that had huge sharp razors sticking out of it. Ashley was sitting on the floor in the corner.

She looked as if she was in a lot of pain and very weak. "Welcome Elizabeth. I see you and your mother made it to our little party after all." Eric said. "Yes we did." I replied. "Its going to be so fun killing you Mary. I've waited so long for this moment." Melina said.

"You're the one who is going to die." Mary replied. "If anyone deserves to die its you!" Melina yelled. "And why is that?" Mary asked. "You are the reason that Will is dead!" Melina said in a furious voice. "As I recall it was your hands that led Will to his final resting place." Mary said in an angry voice.

"It wouldn't have happened if you had just let him be!" Melina yelled. "Will never loved you!" Mary yelled. "Stop!" I yelled. "Melina you are responsible for killing Will. Everything that I have endured is your fault." I said as I walked toward her.

"No. Your mother is to blame and I will make sure that she doesn't leave this cave alive." Melina replied. "Enough!" Eric yelled. "You know this cave is quite strange the way its set up. If I had to guess I would say that there was more to this than meets the eye." I said as I looked around the cave. Eric began to smile. "Clever girl. Your right. There is more to this than meets the eye." Eric yelled.

"Do you want to tell your daughter or should I Mary?" Eric asked. "Tell me what?" I asked looking confused. "Eric has the power of illusion. He can create any illusion he wants any place and anywhere. Eric can also move things with his mind." Mary replied.

"Hardly impressive." I said in a sarcastic voice. "Everyone is entitled to their own opinion." Eric replied with a smile on his face. "Eric this is madness. Let my family and friends go." I pleaded. Eric looked as if he was empty. It was as if he wasn't there at all. Like he didn't have a care in the world.

"For god sakes you have children here! Let them go! I pleaded once more. "Sorry, but you killed my brother and that's something that I don't take lightly." Eric replied. "It wouldn't have happened if he hadn't tried to kill me." I said in a bitter voice.

"You have a human girl that's pregnant with a half vampire child, let her go. She needs medical care." I added. "And she will have it. Olivia was a midwife in her human life." Melina said.

"Your not taking my friend's baby. I won't allow it." I said as I stepped forward ready to fight. "What you want no longer matters!" Melina yelled. "We'll see about that." I replied. As I stood there with Mary I knew that this was it. All hell was about to break loose. It was now or never. The fight was about to begin.

Chapter 17

All Hell Breaks Loose

"Are you ready for this?" I asked as I looked over at Mary. "I'm as ready as I'll ever be." Mary replied. In that moment Melina and Eric began to walk toward us. "What's our plan?" Mary asked. "I'll handle Eric. You take Melina and free the others." In that moment the battle had begun. All hell had broken loose. Eric flew toward me and knocked me back into the wall. Melina came toward Mary and began to fight. I knew that Mary and I would have to fight like hell in order to save the others.

"Give up Elizabeth, you can't win this!" Eric yelled. "Care to bet on that?" I said as I got up off of the floor and ran toward him. As I ran toward Eric I flashed over behind him and caught him by his throat and slammed him down over the chair onto the floor causing the chair to break as well as causing the floor to crack. After that I ran over to free Caleb and Alyssa. It was only a matter of time before Eric would get back up and come at me again.

"Hurry!" Alyssa said in an anxious voice. "I'm trying!" I replied. As I broke the chains with my hands Caleb and Alyssa threw them down on the floor and turned around to free the others. As I turned around I saw Eric getting up.

As he did he looked at me as if he was disgusted and began to run toward me again. As I tried to block Eric's punches I felt his hand on my throat as he pushed me back toward the wall. As I laid on the floor trying to recover so I could move I saw Lex and Athena try to take on. William and Eve followed behind them.

Eric tore them in no time. He ripped their hearts out one by one. They didn't stand a chance. "No!" I screamed. "Mom! Get Ashley out of here!" Shane yelled. Mary ran over and picked Ashley up. She held Ashley in her arms as she ran through us toward the door.

Ashley looked as if she was in a lot of pain. She looked so weak. We were no match for Eric and Melina. They were stronger than Vladimir and Jade were. Olivia on the other hand wasn't so strong. I was taking her out.

"Olivia!" I yelled. Olivia looked at me as I threw the dagger toward her. It only took a minute before the dagger pierced her chest. It was quite a powerful little thing. It went straight through her eart and landed in the wall. "Olivia!" Eric yelled.

"You will pay for this!" Eric said as he flashed over toward Olivia and lifted her body into his arms and ran out of the cave. "Going some where Melina?" I said as I walked toward her. "Not until you and your mother are dead." Melina replied. "I was so hoping you would say that."

As Melina ran toward me I grabbed her in mid air and threw her on to the stone table. Melina arched up as one of the razors pierced her.

"It didn't have to be this way you know." I said as I looked down at her. "You may have won the battle, but my brother will win the war. I'll be waiting for you in the underworld." Melina replied. I lifted the sword and cut her head off.

As I turned around I saw the others standing around the bodies of Eve and her family. As I walked toward their bodies I started to hear the cave sound as if it was about to collapse. "Get their bodies. We will give them a proper funeral." I said as I ran over to get the dagger out of the wall. Caleb, Darren, and Victor grabbed the bodies of Eve's siblings while Benjamin took Eve's body. The cave was about to collapse at any moment. "Go!" I yelled. We ran out of the cave and half way up into the dessert.

When we got far enough away from the cave we all turned around to watch it collapse. Darren and the others set the bodies of our fallen friends down on the ground. "I wish we could have gotten through this without losing anyone." Star said.

"They knew what they were getting theirselves into. We all did." Connor replied. "Its so sad. They were really nice to be vampires." Rosemary said. "They fought bravely. They deserve to be buried with honor. Like the warriors they were." Victor replied.

"Lets bury them then." I said as I started walking down the dessert. "I know a place that we can bury them. Its not far off from here. Its really nice. They will be at peace there." Mary said. "Ashley are you ok?" I asked as we started walking behind Mary.

"Yeah. I have a few pains now and then but nothing major. I feel so weak." Ashley replied. "That's because you need blood. With the baby being half vampire you will need to drink blood every now and then until it arrives." Shane said.

"Alright. Get me some blood vamp boy." Ashley said as she leaned in to kiss Shane. "There's a forest near the place we're going. We can stop there and hunt." Mary said. "Good. I could use a little refreshment. Astarte replied

We walked for about an hour before we entered the forest. Shane caught a deer and drained the blood into his hands so Ashley could drink it. I have to admit, seeing a human drink blood was kind of sigusting.

"Ugh! How do you drink this?" Ashley asked as she wiped the blood off of her lips. "Its in our nature. It's the only way that we can survive. If we don't drink we die." Shane replied. "I guess I have no choice but to get use to it." Ashley said as she leaned down to drink the blood from Shane's hands one again. Ashley is going to adapt to this quicker than I expected. I thought. While the others hunted I went for a walk through the woods.

"Where are you going?" Caleb asked. "For a walk while the others hunt." I replied. "I'll come with you." Caleb said as he put his arm around me. "Wow!" I said as I stumbled over on Caleb. "Are you alright?" Caleb asked.

"Yeah. I just feel dizzy again." I replied. "Maybe you should sit down." I did as Caleb suggested and sat down under the trees. Caleb sat down next to me and put his arm around me. "Why don't you close your eyes and rest." Caleb said as he leaned over and kissed my cheek.

I closed my eyes and laid my head on Caleb's shoulder. As I slept I had another dream. It was completely different. I was running through the woods in a long white dress with Caleb. We were running after a little boy holding a little pirate ship in his hand.

Caleb and I were running and laughing along with the little boy. Then things started to get strange. The little boy moved as we did. He was flashing all around the forest. He smelled like a vampire. I continued to laugh along with Caleb and the little boy.

It was like I was there watching it happen. Finally I caught the little boy and lifted him up into the air as I took him into my arms as we laughed. The boy looked to be about seven years old. Finally the little boy spoke. "Look mommy, I have daddy's pirate ship."

Caleb and I began to laugh. After a moment Caleb began to speak. "Its my gift to you son." The little boy started to laugh again as he began to run through the woods once more as Caleb and I ran behind him flashing all over the forest.

In that moment I woke up to the feeling of someone shaking me. "Elizabeth? Elizabeth, wake up." It was Caleb's voice. "Its time to go." I stood up and brushed the leaves off of my pants. "There's a field not to far from here. We can bury our friends there." Bell said. I nodded and started walking behind them. It only took us about half an hour to get to the field. It was in the clearing of the woods. There were flowers and trees all around.

"This is it." Mary said. Darren and Victor walked toward the field as Benjamin and Caleb followed. They laid the bodies of our fallen friends down and began to rip the ground apart to make a place to bury them. This was truly a sad day for us. We had lost not only good vampires but good friends as well.

It kind of reminded me of when I lost my mother. How the pain of her loss was too much to bare. That same pain returned as I watched Caleb and the others bury Lex and his family.

Chapter 18

A Funeral For Fallen Friends

"Would you like to say a few words, Elizabeth?" Caleb asked as he and the others walked toward us. "I would be glad to." I replied as I stepped forward. "They were our brave soldiers and loving friends. Having to go on without them is going to be hard. They were some of the best vampires that we ever knew. In the end they fought for what they believed in as well as fighting for total strangers that they knew for only a short time. I will miss you my friends. I pray that you are in a good place and are at last at peace. May you be rewarded with everlasting love and kindness for your bravery on this journey."

I felt a tear of blood fall down my face. I may not of known these vampires for long but in the short time that we had together I felt as if they were part of my family. I would not only miss them, but I would never forget them.

"I would like to say something if that's alright." Ashley said. "Of course." Amelia replied. "I know that I don't know any of you that well, but I have to admit that none of you are like what I imagined. I thought that vampires were pure evil creatures that cared about nothing except blood and killing to survive but you all are different."

Ashley took a deep breath and continued "You all take life because if you don't you will die and at first that scared me, but after getting to know all of you I've realized that none of you asked for this. It was given to you against your will. None of you had a choice in the matter." Suddenly Amelia stepped forward to speak.

"Some of us had a choice. Some of us chose this so that we wouldn't have to face death." Ashley smiled and took Amelia's hand as if she was trying to give Amelia a sudden feeling of comfort. After a moment Ashley started to speak again. "I guess what I'm trying to say is that even though I only knew your friends for a short time I grew to like them. I've also grown to like all of you as well." Everyone began to smile.

"Thank you." Bell said. "No. Thank you. You have all taught me to trust the soul of a person rather than the look of them." Ashley replied. "Soul? We don't have a soul." Darren said as he looked at Ashley confused. Amelia nudged Darren in the arm.

"She knows that! Your going to ruin the moment shut up!" Amelia said as she put her hand over Darren's mouth. Everyone started to smile again. "I guess that wasn't the right choice of words beings that you all have no soul." Ashley said as she started to look embarrassed.

"Its ok. You did good." I said as I smiled and put my arm around her. "Yeah. Good speech." Mason said. "I have one more thing that I would like to say." Ashley said as she started to look serious. "Alright." I replied. "Shane would you come and stand beside me?" Ashley asked. As Shane stood beside Ashley I started to get a little nervous. I wondered what she was going to say.

After a moment Ashley began to speak. "I know that all of you are probably against me becoming one of you, and I understand that. I know that I'm about to get into a lot here. I just want all of you to know that this is my decision and I'm making it based on my love for Shane as well as our child." It was true. I didn't want Ashley becoming one of us in the beginning because I knew of the consequences that becoming one of us would hold.

It was frightening for me to think of the animal that Ashley would become as well as the pain of having her soul ripped apart from her body. To live with no soul is far more worse than death.

I would give anything to have mine back, but unfortunately that's not possible. I am what I was made and I come as I come. There's no magic pill for this. There's only eternity.

"We all support the decision that you make. I was against your choice that you were making as well as what would await you after the change was made." I said.

"I'm well aware of the consequences." Ashley replied. "I know you are. I just hope that you can live with them." In that moment Shane began to speak. "I'm going to be the one to change Ashley after the baby is born. I won't make you carry te pain of having to change your best friend into a monster. That's something that I'm prepared to live with." I looked at Shane with remorse. "Its not that I couldn't live with changing Ashley into a monster Shane. Its taking her soul that I can't live with." I replied.

"We need to start tracking Eric." Mary said. "He'll be after us soon." Mary added. "I agree. We need to get to him before he gets to us." Bradley replied. "What's the plan?" Ashley asked. "We need to follow Eric's scent and find him. Its going to take all of us to bring him down." I told them. "Eric is very powerful. He has a lot of powers. I could feel them when I was around him." Alyssa said.

"Your powers are beginning to kick in." Amelia replied. Suddenly Alyssa looked as if she was disturbed by something. "What's wrong

Alyssa?" I asked. "I can hear Eric's thoughts." Alyssa replied. "From here?" I asked suddenly amazed. "Yes. He's going to the city of Alexandria." Alyssa replied. "How did you know that my powers were starting to kick in?" Alyssa asked as she looked at Amelia confused. "I could sense them." Amelia replied.

"Eric is going to Templeton Castle." Bell said as she looked as if she was having a vision. "Do you know where that is?" I asked. "No." Bell replied. "I do. Its in Alexandria." Astarte replied. "I'll lead you there." Astarte added. "Eric isn't far from here. We can probably find him before he gets to Alexandria." Alyssa said.

"Good girl." Amelia replied. "Lets start tracking. I'm in the mood for some adventure." Mason said. As we began to track Eric I knew that this would be the most dangerous thing that we had done in a long time. Something told me that this wasn't going to be easy. Things were about to get a lot harder.

I felt like I was going into a suicide mission with my family. Eric was much more powerful than Vladimir was. Truth be told I think Eric is far more worse than Julian ever was. With Eric being able to create illusions as well as move things with his mind I knew that we would be on a dangerous mission. It was a mission as well as a chance that I had to take. Eric was a threat to my family and I had to take him out.

In some strange way I feel like that even though I didn't know Will I owed him this. Julian and Melina were already gone. Now Eric was all that was left of the murderous trio. I felt as if I needed to avenge Will's death by killing the last of the trio. I guess I felt that once Eric was dead that Will would be at peace and Mary could finally have some peace in her eternal life.

I never thought that I would say this but I guess I'm doing this for them. Two strangers that I barely even know that are my real parents that I never knew I had until now. My real creators. The two creators that gave me life. It was simple now. I knew my path. Eric had to die and I was the one who would deliver the swift hand of justice once again.

Chapter 19

Tracking Eric

Eric's scent was leading me down a straight path through the woods. I knew I was close to catching him, but I also knew that he was clever too. I knew that Eric would have some sort of trap that he would lay ahead of us in order to slow us down. It was just a matter of time before we fell into it. I was prepared though. I was ready for anything that Eric was going to throw at me. Come hell or high water I would over come any obstacles that were in our path.

"Eric's scent is strong. I know we're close to him." I said as I kept walking with the others. "Eric may be leading us on the right path but he's definitely got a trap set for us." Alyssa said. "How do you know that?" Mason asked. "I can hear it in his mind." Alyssa replied.

"Eric is counting on us to walk into his trap." Amelia said. "What is the trap?" I asked. "I don't know. Eric isn't saying anything about it except that he can't wait for us to come across it." Alyssa replied. "Bell, can you see what it is?" Caleb asked.

"No. I can't control when the visions come to me. I can only see them when they appear and try to change the outcomes." Bell replied. "We're like the prey to a predator." Ashley said as she walked behind us with Shane. "Looks like it." Shane replied. "Lets just keep walking and follow Eric's scent." I told them.

We kept walking east following Eric's scent until we got to a clearing where we saw a field. The field looked exactly like my dream. There was flowers everywhere along with a water fall on the other side of the field.

I couldn't believe it. My dreams were real. "What is it Elizabeth?" Caleb asked. "This is it. This is the place from my dream." I replied as I walked forward and looked around. "Why would Eric's scent lead me here?" I asked as I looked around the field once again. "I don't know. He's clever." Caleb replied. "Its an illusion." Alyssa said. "What?" I said in disbelief.

"Eric is near by. I can sense him." Alyssa replied as she started to look around. "Eric can read a person's mind when he is in the physical presence of someone. This would explain the field that we are seeing." Mary said. Suddenly Bell looked as if she was having a vision. "What is it?" Amelia asked as she put her hand on Bell's shoulder.

"There's something else here. I don't know what it is but its not good." Bell replied. "What are you seeing?" Benjamin asked. "I see souls. So many souls." Bell stopped and gasped as if she was really disturbed by something. "There coming!" Bell yelled.

In that moment I looked around and saw that we were surrounded by humans. Dead humans. They looked like they were in so much pain. "What's going on?" Pandora asked. "We're seeing human victims from our past!" Bell replied.

Suddenly I looked across the field to see Eric standing near the waterfall.

"Face your past!" Eric yelled. "These are the victims of your animalistic nature Let them torture you all like you all tortured my family!" Eric added as he began to laugh. The human souls were closing in on us. We were all standing around in a circle. "What do we do?" Raven asked.

"Take the children and get them to safety." I replied. "Come on Pandora!" Raven yelled as she jumped up in the air and flew toward the waterfall with Sky in her arms. Pandora followed behind her with Serenity.

"Shane take Ashley and follow Raven." I told him. Shane nodded and picked Ashley up into his arms and jumped over the humans and headed toward Raven and the others. "What do we do now?" Connor asked. "We have no choice but to fight them." I replied. "I don't want to harm them." Amelia said.

"We have no choice! We have to fight!" Darren yelled. "Just fight through them!" I yelled. "Wait! This is just an illusion remember? Make peace with them and they'll leave!" Alyssa yelled. "Are you kidding me? We killed them! Why would they want to make peace with us?" Phillip asked.

"Its not for us! Its for them!" Alyssa yelled. "Eric is controlling them with his mind. That's another one of his gifts. Do what Alyssa says! Its our only chance!" Mary yelled. We all began to try and make peace with the dead humans that were before us.

"What we did to you was wrong. We would take it back if we could, but we can't." Amelia said. The humans stopped closing in on us. They started to back up. I started to look around as they began to scatter. "Well that was easy." I said looking surprised.

As I looked over at Eric he looked as if he was furious by something. "What are you doing? You were all suppose to kill them you fools!" Eric yelled in a furious voice. As I looked at the humans I noticed that all of them were looking at Alyssa.

Alyssa was standing there in the middle of the circle with her eyes closed. "Alyssa?" I said as I walked toward her. "She's telling the humans to move on into the next world." Amelia said. "She's in their minds?" I asked looking amazed. "Yes." Amelia replied.

"Alyssa just tapped into another one of her powers." Bell said. "Its about time." Darren replied. With in a few minutes the humans began to disappear into thin air. They just faded away into a bright ball of light. "I guess they finally found their peace." Star said. "Yes they did. We gave it to them." Alyssa replied as she opened her eyes.

"Is that all you got?!" I yelled as I looked over at Eric and began to walk toward the waterfall. "Oh no my dear. I have much more in store for you. Much more." Eric replied as he turned around and ran through the woods. "Come on everyone. Eric will get a good head start on us if we don't hurry up and follow him." I said as I began to run toward the woods.

When I got into the woods I stopped running and waited for the others to catch up. As I waited for the others I saw the place in my dream begin to fade away. As the flowers and the waterfall disappeared I saw nothing but dead trees and dirt. Just another part of the forest.

When the others caught up with me we started following Eric's scent once again. This time Eric was heading west. We knew that he was heading for Alexandria. It was only a matter of time before Eric would make it to Templeton Castle where he would be waiting for us. We were like mice following bread crumbs as far as Eric was concerned. After walking through the woods for a few hours I heard Ashley moan.

"What is it Ashley? I said as I turned around to look at her. "Just a pain. I feel like I'm being stabbed." Ashley replied as she leaned over on Shane. Before I could say anything Ashley started to scream. "Ah!"

"What's wrong with her?" I asked in a panicked voice as I looked over at Bell. "Its Eric. He's using his powers to inflict physical pain on Ashley so she will go into labor early." Bell replied. "He can do that?" I asked as I looked over at Mary. "Yes." Mary replied. "We need to take Ashley to the oracle in Rosetta. She will know what to do." Mary added.

"Alright. We'll go to Rosetta and then we'll head to Alexandria." I replied. "How far is Alexandria from Rosetta?" I asked. "It's right before Alexandria." Mary replied. "Once we get Ashley seen about we'll go to Alexandria and take care of Eric." I said. "Come on love. Lets get your friend to the oracle." Caleb said. Caleb and I walked beside Shane and Ashley in case she started having more pains.

I wanted to catch Eric first and get him out of the way but Ashley was more important. I had to get her taken care of first. I couldn't let anything happen to my best friend. I wouldn't forgive myself if anything ever did. No, Eric would have to wait. Getting to the oracle was much more important. Ashley's life depended on it.

Chapter 20

The Oracle Of Rosetta

We had walked all day and finally came to the city of Rosetta. The moon was high in the sky and the air was settling all around us like a cool blanket. Ashley looked completely exhausted. Poor dear, I felt sorry for her. I could only imagine what she must be going through. Sadly I'll never know. Vampires can't have children unfortunately. As we entered the city or Rosetta we saw a temple made out of gold setting in the middle of a dessert. The city wasn't too far off behind it. We were only a few miles out from it. I grabbed Ashley's hand as we began making our way toward the temple.

"We're almost there Ashley." I said as I held Ashley's hand to help her along the way. Ashley was starting to feel dizzy. Shane and I walked on each side of her to make sure that she didn't fall over. "Hopefully the oracle will have something for the pain." Mary said.

"Don't worry the oracle will be able to help her. Ashley won't have the baby until the eclipse." Bell replied. "The eclipse?" I said looking confused. There will be an eclipse when the baby is born. It will mark the baby's coming into the world." Bell replied. "There's always an eclipse when a hybrid is born. I don't know why." Mary said,

"The eclipse is meant to be the symbol between dark and light.

Because hybrids are made from vampires and humans the eclipse is the symbol that marks their entry into the world. For vampires are dark and humans are considered light." Astarte replied.

"Well that makes since." Mary said. "Now I know why I saw an eclipse when Shane was born." Mary added. "So tell me about this oracle of Rosetta. What's she like?" Ashley asked. "The oracle is a vampire of course, but she's very kind. Bradley brought me to her before Shane was born." Mary replied.

"Will she try to eat me?" Ashley asked with a slight smile on her face as she tried to keep her mind off of the pain. "No. Believe it or not it is against the oracle's vows to harm humans." Mary replied. "How does she survive if she doesn't feed on humans?" I asked looking curious.

"The oracle feeds strictly on synthetic blood." Bradley replied. "So it is possible to go with out feeding on humans?" I asked in a hopeful voice. "Yes." Bradley replied. "Huh? That's funny. I thought we would get sick and eventually die if we didn't feed on human blood." I said as I looked over at Caleb. "Before you even start I didn't know that." Caleb replied as he looked at me pointing his finger toward me.

"Well now you know." I said with a slight smile. "Fight later children. I need drugs." Ashley said. As we came closer to the city of Rosetta I saw what looked to be Egyptian symbols engraved all over the oracle's temple. I didn't know what they meant but the way they were engraved on the temple walls simply fascinated me.

For once there were no guards. That seemed rather strange to me. I looked over at Ashley as I stood there with the others in front of the temple doors. "Are you ready to go inside?" I asked. "Do I have a choice?" Ashley said as she looked at me with a slight smile. "Don't worry love. You will be fine." Shane said.

"As long as I'm with you I'm not worried." Ashley replied. As we walked inside the temple there were more symbols written on the walls.

In the center of the room was a tall golden chair. Just below the chair was a silver table made out of marble. On each side of the chair stood two women. They weren't human though. They weren't even vampires.

They were something else. One had long blonde hair and brown amber colored eyes along with a white dress. The other woman had long black hair and hazel colored eyes along with a black dress. "Who are they?" I asked as I looked over at Mary.

"They are the protectors of the oracle." Mary replied. "The one in the white stands for peace and all things that are good in the world. The one in the black stands for chaos and all the things in the world that are evil." Bradley said. "Why does the oracle need them?" I asked.

"About a century after I discovered that I was the first vampire to ever be on the earth I also discovered two guardians. The guardian of good who is know as Isis and the guardian of evil who is known as Brigit.

The prophecy of time is also protected by the guardians. It is the prophecy that for told of a human girl that would have the gift of being able to see all and know all." Astarte replied.

"Which would be the oracle right?" I asked. "Yes. When the oracle was discovered by the guardians as the one who was for told in the prophecy of time it was then decided that both sides would protect the one who sees all and knows all. That being the oracle of Rosetta." Astarte replied.

"I may have been the first vampire to ever be on this earth but the guardians have been here since time began. They are the only ones who are older than I am." Astarte added. "How did the oracle become a vampire?" I asked.

"Well that's how I met the guardians. They told me of an oracle in the city of Rosetta who had unlimited power. They wanted me to turn the oracle so that she could use her powers through out time." Astarte explained.

"My family and I may be the oldest vampires on earth but the oracle is not too far behind us." Astarte added. "Welcome." Isis said. "Why have you all come?" Brigit asked. "We are here to see the oracle. This human is pregnant with a hybrid child." Astarte replied.

"Wait here. I will get the oracle." Isis said as she began to walk back toward a door. "It has been a long time Astarte." Brigit said. "Yes it has." Astarte replied. After a few moments Isis returned. "The oracle will see you now." Isis said. In that moment the oracle came out through the door and began to walk toward the golden chair. As the oracle walked toward the chair she looked at me and smiled.

The oracle was very pretty. She had long curly strawberry colored hair and greenish gold eyes and was very tiny. The oracles robes were quite beautiful. They were white with a golden coat that came to the floor. "I am told that you have a human who is pregnant with a hybrid child." The oracle said as she sat down on the golden chair.

"Yes. The human is having extreme pain and is rather weak due to her condition." Astarte replied. "I assume you have told your friends when the baby will come?" The oracle asked as she looked over at Bell. "Yes. I have told them of the child's coming." Bell replied.

"Yes. You have also neglected to mention another matter. However, I can see that you and the others have plans to tell of that matter when the time comes." The oracle said as she looked over at me and smiled.

I just looked back at her with a confused look. I had no idea what the oracle was talking about. "All in good time." Caleb replied with a slight smile. Now I knew that something was up. "Put the human on the table so I can examine her." The oracle said. Shane and I brought Ashley toward the table and laid her down as the oracle got up out of her chair and walked forward.

Shane and I stepped back with the others so that the oracle could examine Ashley. It was kind of interesting to watch the oracle. She moved with such grace to be a vampire. I watched as the oracle placed her hands on top of Ashley's stomach.

Ashley's stomach was as big as a watermelon. I kind of smiled at that thought. Ashley remained still while the oracle moved her hands around her stomach. The oracle had her eyes closed as if she was seeing something. After a moment the oracle began to smile and opened her eyes.

"Your going to have a healthy son. He will stop aging when he is seventeen. Your son will also have strong powers." The oracle said. "A son!" Shane said in an excited voice as he leaned down to kiss Ashley's forehead.

"Your son will have unimaginable strength and speed. He will get that from his father. As far as your son's other powers he will get those from you." The oracle said. "Powers? What powers?" Shane asked. "Ashley is a witch. Remember?" I replied. "Oh yeah." Shane replied.

"You can sit up now Ashley. I will give you some mandrake root for the pain." The oracle said as she walked back toward the door. As the oracle went to get the mandrake root for Ashley's pain Astarte began to talk to the guardians.

"I wish we could have came her under different circumstances." Astarte said. "As do we." Isis replied. "It has been delightful to see you again." Brigit said with a slight smile. "I'm sure it has." Connor muttered in a low voice. Rosemary nudged Connor in the arm. In that moment the oracle came out of the back room holding the mandrake root in her hand.

I stood next to Ashley while Shane kept his arm around her in case she got dizzy again. "Here is the mandrake root." The oracle said. "Every time you start to feel a pain I want you to put a little in your mouth and chew on it in order to numb your pain." The oracle added. "The child inside you is growing like a weed." Isis said as she began to smile. "You should be ready to give birth in no time." Brigit said.

"I'm ready." Ashley replied as she put her hand on her stomach. "I hope so. Your in for more than you know." The oracle said as she looked down at Ashley's stomach. "What do you mean?" Ashley asked looking worried. "The child with in you is going to have some pretty strong powers beings that you are a witch." The oracle replied.

"What kind of powers?" Shane asked. "As soon as the child stops aging he will come into his powers. He will be able to astral project, and have a strength unlike any other vampire before him. Your son will be the strongest vampire yet. Your son will be able to do everything that Ashley can do." The oracle replied.

Ashley looked at the oracle as if she was rather pleased and amazed. "That's how I got my powers." Ashley said. "I inherited my powers from my mother. I have the ability to send messages out to others through meditation as well as read a persons future by their palm. I can also cast spells and create barriers to protect others." Ashley added.

"Fascinating." Astarte said. "Yes it is." Isis agreed. "Your visit is much appreciated but you must all leave now if you hope to catch up with Eric soon." The oracle said. "Beware of the trap that Eric has set for you when you reach the city of Alexandria. It will not be like the last." The oracle added.

"What is it?" I asked looking worried. "Its not good. All of your will lose your lives if your not careful." The oracle replied. "Proceed with caution." Isis said. "Always be prepared for the unexpected." Brigit said. "And so we shall be." Connor replied. "We will watch out for anything that looks suspicious." Caleb said. "Looks like I'm going to have put my hunting instincts to use." Amelia said.

"We all will." Alyssa replied. "I'm ready for whatever lays ahead." Mason said. "You still have a lot to learn my friend." Victor replied as he put his hand on Mason's shoulder. "Be safe on your journey my friends. Do come again." The oracle said.

We all turned around and began to walk toward the golden doors. As we got outside of the temple I stood there for a moment. "What's wrong?" Alyssa asked. "Something doesn't feel right." I replied. "What do you mean?" Mary asked looking worried. "I just have a bad feeling about what's going to happen when we reach Alexandria." I said as I put my hand on my forehead.

"I know. We're all headed into a trap but we can't let Eric scare us away. We can't let him win. We have to beat him." Mary replied. "Your right. Lets get to Alexandria and end this." I said as I reached out to put my hand on Mary's shoulder.

As we began to head to Alexandria I knew that whatever laid ahead was going to be tough but I also knew that we could get through it. We had to. Otherwise Lex and his family would have died for nothing. Their death would be in vain if we didn't keep fighting.

There was no way that I was about to give up. Even though I hated that our friends were gone I would do everything in my power to stop Eric. I would do what I had to in order to take him out. Even if it mean that I had to die in order to ensure that Eric never harmed another living soul or another friend of mine ever again.

Yes, I would see Eric fall. I would see him dead for all of the pain that he caused my family and I, but most of all I would see Eric suffer in his final moments when he and I met again.

Eric would pay for the pain that he and his family inflicted on Mary and Will along with the others that I have lost along the way. In my mind Eric and his family were the ones who started all of this.

In my mind I felt as if they were the ones who were really responsible for the life that I've had to live in the dark and cold wastelands of eternity. Yes, for this I would see Eric perish and I would enjoy every minute of it. Tonight I take revenge and with that revenge I take a life.

I take the life of a soul that is just as damned as my own. Tonight I pay whatever cost to see this done. Even if the cost is my own life.

Chapter 21

City Of Alexandria

As we entered the city of Alexandria I knew that things were about to get ugly. No matter. I would welcome the challenge. I would take anything that Eric threw at me and turn it inside out only to see the mad expression of fury fill up with in his face. I would do everything that I could to make Eric as angry as possible. Tonight was the night where the winner would take all and that winner was going to be me. For I would take all. I would take anything that Eric dished out and then some. It was time to get proactive. It was time for me to become the monster that I had always feared of becoming.

It was time to become evil. Ruthless. It was time for me to sink straight down to Eric's level. I had to become the creature that I was made to be. A vampire. Not just any vampire though. I had to become a ruthless, evil, not a care in the world about anything vampire.

As the others and I kept walking into the city I could see the Templeton castle. We were only a few miles out from it. From what I could see the castle looked like a dark 11th century type of castle. It was black as night.

In my opinion the castle looked like the scum of the earth. It looked like it was just dead. Like it had sucked the life out of everything around it. The castle was like a place of death. As we kept walking Ashley started to have some more pains.

"Here chew on some mandrake root." Shane said as he took a piece out of the white cloth and put it in Ashley's mouth. "Don't worry Ash, this will all be over before you know it." I told her as I put my hand on her shoulder.

I kept walking with the others as we made our way to Templeton castle. Suddenly I came to a stop. I began to smell something fowl. It smelled like rotten eggs. It was horrible. The smell was so strong. "What is that awful smell?" Ashley asked. "How can you smell it?" Shane asked. "Pregnant women smell everything." Mary replied. "I don't know what it is but it smells like rotten eggs." I said as I started to look around.

"Whatever it is its close." Amelia said. "Get ready. Whatever it is will be popping out soon enough." Benjamin replied. "Pandora get the children to safety. Raven said. "Don't worry I got them." Pandora replied as she moved over near a tree with her arms round the children.

"Elizabeth do you still have that dagger?" Mary asked. "Yes." I replied. "Why?" I asked. "Because if the smell in the air is the scent of what I think it is your going to need it." Mary replied.

I took the dagger out and held it in my hand. I was ready for whatever was about to happen. In that moment I heard something moving through the trees. "Its getting close." Mary said. "Everyone get ready." Astarte said. After a moment the creature moved out from behind the trees.

All of us looked up at it as our bodies went stiff. It was ten feet tall. It's tail was about five foot long. It was a copper looking color and its eyes were brown. It was a scorpion. The stinger on the tail was about three foot long and the pinchers looked to be about two feet wide.

I knew we were in deep trouble now. "We're in trouble." Darren said in a low voice. "You read my mind." I said with a slight smile on my face. "Funny." Darren replied as he kept his eyes on the creature that was approaching us. "This must be the trap that the oracle was talking about." Ashley said. "Yep." I replied as I held the dagger close to my side.

"Shane, take Ashley and go over by Pandora." I told him. "So Mary, whats the name of this creature?" I asked. "Larva. He's another one of Eric's pets." Mary replied. In that moment Larva began to strike with one of his claws. We all scattered about trying to surround him.

"Pandora, take Ashley and the kids into the woods. We'll meet you soon." I said. As Pandora fled off with the children Shane took Ashley and started running behind her. "Marry! Catch!" I yelled. I threw the dagger toward Mary and ripped up a tree stump from out of the ground and held it in my hands.

"What are you doing?" Mary asked. "I'm going to have a little fun." I said with a slight grin. As Larva tried to strike me with the stinger at the end of his tail I threw the tree stump toward him. As the tree stump hit him Larva flew back through two other buildings in the city.

There were no humans around. The city was deserted. "We need to come up with a game plan while Larva is down." Mary said. "I've got a plan." I replied. "What is it?" Astarte asked. "We need to get to Templeton castle. I propose that we make a run for it." I replied. "Larva will get up any minute. He will come after us." Bell said. "I know. That's why we have to distract him if we hope to reach the castle." I replied.

"Take the others and go to the castle. Victor and I can distract Larva long enough for you to make it. After that we will go to Pandora and the others and come at the castle from the back way." Caleb said. "No. we need to take Larva out." I replied. You and Victor round up Pandora and the others and meet us at the castle. In the mean time the rest of us will distract Larva while we make a run for the castle." I said.

"OK. Be careful." Caleb said as he leaned in to press his lips against mine. Star leaned in to kiss Victor before he turned around and started to run behind Caleb. As Caleb and Victor fled the others and I started to run toward the castle.

"Larva is coming! We have to hurry!" Amelia yelled. "Don't worry we'll make it!" I yelled as I kept running toward the castle. Larva was catching up to us. I had to take him out and I had to do it now if the others and I stood any chance at getting to the castle before Larva could pick us off like pieces on a game board. I began to yell at the others behind me. "I'm going to distract Larva! The rest of you get to the castle and hurry!" I yelled.

"What about you?!" Alyssa yelled. "I'll be fine! Now go!" I yelled as I broke out from the others and began to turn and run toward Larva. Larva was coming at me fast. I had to think of something quickly if I wanted to avoid colliding with him.

I began to flash around from one spot to the next in order to confuse Larva. As I turned around to run back toward Larva he reached out with one of his claws and tried to catch me. I flashed around him and leaped through the air toward the castle.

Larva was angry now. I jumped from house to house flashing around so fast that not even Larva could keep up with me. I used all of the strength and energy I had to out run hum. As I came closer to the castle I saw the others standing in front of it watching as I ran toward them as Larva was beginning to catch up to me.

As I reached the entrance of the castle where the others stood I turned around. "Elizabeth, what are you doing?!" Bradley yelled. "You'll see!" I yelled back. "Don't worry Elizabeth. I've got you covered." Alyssa said as she walked up beside me. "What are you going to do?" I asked. "You'll see." Alyssa replied with a grin on her face.

"Wait for it." Alyssa said as we stood there waiting for Larva to get closer. "Wait for it." Alyssa said once again as we continued to wait. As soon as Larva was with in three feet of us Alyssa turned around and yelled at the others. "Move!" Alyssa yelled. I stood next to Alyssa to protect her. In that moment as Larva was about to close in on us Alyssa was standing still as if she was concentrating hard on something.

In that moment I saw a pyramid being lifted up into the air. It flew across toward Larva and landed on top of him. As the pyramid landed on top of Larva it crushed him like a bug. He was no more. As far as I was concerned he was one giant dead monster.

As Alyssa and I turned around and walked toward the others I started to feel dizzy again. Instead of stumbling this time I fell toward the ground on my knees. "Elizabeth!" Alyssa yelled in a panicked voice as she knelt down to try and help me up. "I'm alright. I'm just dizzy." I replied. "You shouldn't be doing all of this fighting." Alyssa said in an irritated voice.

"Relax! I'm a vampire remember?" I said with a slight smile on my face. "You may be a vampire but you need to be careful." Alyssa said as she put her hand to my face. "Your burning up again." Alyssa added. "What's the big deal? Larva is dead. I said as I looked at Alyssa with a confused look. "Its more of a bid deal than you think!" Alyssa snapped.

"What?" I asked looking confused once again. "Your---." Alyssa stopped speaking in that moment. It was as if she wanted to say something but she couldn't. "Its just that you've been dizzy for a while now and we still haven't figured out what's wrong with you." Star said as if she was trying to cover up whatever it was that Alyssa was about to say.

"Well I'm fine. I appreciate the concern but I'm fine. So lets get in there and take Eric down." I replied as I stood up on my feet. "Are you sure your ok?" Alyssa asked looking worried. "Peachy." I said with a smile. "Funny." Alyssa replied. "Caleb and the others should be here soon. Lets get inside and start looking for Eric." Raven said. As we entered the Templeton castle I knew that there would be more traps laid out for us. It was only a matter of time before we walked right into them.

What could Eric have for us next? I thought. What monster would we face this time? Truth be told I enjoyed the challenge of facing his supernatural creatures but enough was enough. It was time to get down to business. Enough of the games. It was time to be serious.

I was ready for the final battle. The war to end all wars. It was time to face each other like two warriors on a battlefield. Winner takes all. I was ready to make Eric the full recipient of my rage. I wanted him to be the main target of my anger. It was time for Eric to suffer for all of the pain that he had caused.

It was time for him to be the victim for once. Yes, it was time for the roles to be reversed. It was time for Eric to be the victim and of me to be the bully. Like the predator seeking out its prey. It was time for me to become the predator and for Eric to become the prey.

It was time for me to become the hunter and for Eric to become the hunted. Yes, this was it. My moment. All of the events that have taken place since Will was killed have been leading up to this moment. After all, Eric and his family were the ones who were responsible for the things that had happened in my life.

They took away my chance at being able to get to know where I really came from. This life that I had now was all because of them. When they killed my real father and therefore forced Mary to give me away they set everything in motion as of that night.

Yes, if anyone was going to die tonight it was Eric. It was time to finish what he and his family started. It was time for me to not only become the creature that I had always feared of becoming, but it was time for me to become something far worse.

It was time for me to become evil.

Chapter 22

Templeton Castle

As I entered the castle with the others I began to look around for Eric. It was too quiet and the castle was really dark. Of course, we could still see where we were going but the darkness of the castle made me even more cautious. "Something's not right." I said as I continued walking around the castle with the others. "Everything's fine. Eric likes darkness and decay." Mary replied. "So that's the fowl stench in the air." I said as I kept walking. "Eric's close. I can smell him." Bradley said. As we kept walking I could smell Caleb and the others. As I looked on down the hall I saw what looked to be a light.

As the others and I got closer I could see that it was Caleb holding a torch in front of Shane and Ashley. Pandora and the children stood next to them. "It smells so bad in here." Ashley said. "You can smell it too?" Shane asked looking amazed.

"Pregnant women." Mary said shrugging her shoulders. "Yeah. Right. Well from the smell of things I would say that Eric isn't too far off." Shane replied. "There's a tower on up from here. If we follow the stairs we should catch up with Eric soon." Bradley said.

"Lets go." Ashley said. "Where do you think your going?" I asked as I put my hand on Ashley's shoulder. "With you." Ashley replied.

"Ashley its not safe for you to be going with us in your condition." I told her. "I don't care. You're my best friend. I'll be fine." Ashley replied.

I couldn't help but to admire Ashley's bravery. "Besides, I've got you and Shane to protect me right?" Ashley said as she put her hand on my shoulder. "You know you do." I replied as I put my hand on Ashley's shoulder. "You have all of us." Caleb said.

"Definitely." Connor replied. "Why Connor, I didn't think you liked us that much." I said in a teasing voice as I began to smile. "You all may be a pain at times but your all actually not that bad." Connor replied. "If any of you ever give me any grief over my sudden kindness I will hunt you all down and tear you apart." Connor added with a devious smile. "Your charm is so lovely." I teased.

Connor suddenly game me a slight smile. "Now lets do this." Connor said. "Wait. We need to find a place where the children will be safe. I can't worry about little Serenity and Sky while I'm fighting along side the rest of you." Pandora said.

"Your not." Astarte replied. "Astarte I love you, but don't tell me what I'm not going to do." Pandora said as she began to look at Astarte with furious eyes. "I'm not trying to tell you what to do but you are my wife and its my job to protect you." Astarte replied.

"And what is my job?" Pandora asked as began to look even more furious. "Is it not my job to do the same for you?" Pandora asked. Astarte was silent for a moment. He looked as if he was thinking of what to say. After a moment he spoke. "Yes. Yes it is, but I am your husband and I refuse to put you in any danger."

Pandora began to look furious. "So let me get this straight, you can out yourself in danger for me, but I can't put myself in danger for you?" Pandora asked. "No, I refuse to let you put yourself at risk." Astarte replied.

"You refuse!" Pandora said in an angry voice. "Astarte I am not some human that you can order around! I am your wife!" Pandora started to look even more angry.

"That's why I am telling you this. I don't want you to get hurt." Astarte replied. "Look all of us standing around here while you two fuss is not getting us any closer to Eric." I said as I made my way passed them.

"What's our plan?" Astarte asked. "Simple. We go in there and kill that monster." I replied. "Its not that simple." Caleb said. "Yes it is." Mason replied. "Oh really and how is that?" Caleb asked.

"With all of us here there's no way that we can lose." Mason replied. "You are so young." Victor said shaking his head. "Lead the way Mary." I said. As Mary started to lead us up toward the tower I began to have a bad feeling. I hated having these feelings. Every time I had them something bad always happened.

The stairs were just as black as the castle. It was dark and gloomy as we walked up the steps. Mary, Victor, Astarte, and I carried a torch to light the way. We grabbed them from the wall that led up toward the tower. As we came closer to the tower I started to smell Eric. I could also smell something else. It was fowl. Like the smell of new death only it smelled like many new deaths. "What is that awful smell?" I asked.

"Vampires. Newborn vampires." Astarte replied. "Oh great." I said in a sarcastic voice. As the others and I approached the double black doors at the end of the stairs Astarte began to speak. "This is going to be a tough battle everyone. The toughest one that I think that we have faced yet. Be prepared fir anything."

"That's right. Eric is very smart." Mary replied. "Beware of his illusions. He can use them to trick you as well as use them to mess with your mind." Bradley said. Astarte turned around to kiss Pandora. "This is where we part company my love." Astarte said.

"Why won't you let me fight with you?" Pandora asked. "I've already told you." Astarte replied. "I'm your wife. I should be fighting by your side instead of hiding in the shadows." Pandora said as she reached out to touch Astarte's face.

"I understand your point love, but because you are my wife as well as the mother of my child I need you to stay behind. Its like I've told you before, if anything happens to me you must take care of our child." Astarte said as he ran his fingers through Pandora's hair.

"You are such a stubborn man." Pandora replied with a slight smile. "Yeah but you know I'm only stubborn because I love you so much." Astarte said. "I'll see you soon my little sweet girl." Raven said as she leaned down to wrap her arms around Sky.

"Mommy will the fighting ever stop so we can be together?" Sky asked. "One day sweet heart. I promise." Raven replied. Sky walked toward Pandora. Serenity reached out to hold Sky's hand while Pandora placed her hands on their shoulders.

"Here we go again." Raven said with a slight smile as she walked toward Pandora. "Yep." Pandora replied. "I really appreciate you looking out for my daughter." Raven said.

"She's like my own." Pandora replied. "Maybe next time you can go kick but and I can babysit." Raven teased. "Maybe so." Pandora replied. Raven hugged Pandora and turned around to come and stand beside me. "Ashley you need to go with Pandora." Shane said. "No I'm not leaving you." Ashley replied.

"Its not safe for you to be near Eric in your present condition. He'll kill you." Shane pleaded. "What about you?" Ashley asked as she reached out to put her hand on Shane's face. "Don't worry about me. I'll be fine." Shane replied. "I love you." Ashley said.

"I love you too." Shane said as he leaned forward to kiss Ashley on the lips. "Now go." Shane said. "I'll go with Pandora and help keep Ashley and the children safe." Beth said. "Thank you." I told her. Pandora flashed down the stairs with the children to wait for our return. Beth grabbed Ashley's hand and led her down the stairs holding a torch. "This is it." Alyssa said.

"Is everyone ready?" I asked. Everyone nodded as I began to open the doors. As we walked into the room it was empty. The room was just as dark as the rest of the castle even though there were torches lit all around.

The floors were black. There was a row of black stairs. There was a black chair at the top of the stairs and a black statue on each side of the chair that looked to be gargoyles. "I thought that gargoyles were meant to rid off evil?" Alyssa asked. "Well apparently not." Mason replied.

"This was too easy. I don't like it." I said. "I agree." Amelia replied. "Eric's here and so are his little minions. Their just in hiding." Mary said. "Come out Eric! I know you're here!" Mary yelled. Suddenly I heard a laugh. It was Eric. I was sure of it. With in a moment Eric appeared and with him were a whole room full of vampires. Newborn vampires.

We were all instantly surrounded by them. Thirty of them all together. "I'm so glad you could all make it. I've been waiting for you all to show up." Eric said with a slight smile. "Wouldn't miss it." I replied in a sarcastic voice.

"I take it these are your minions?" I asked. "Well, aren't you the clever girl? Yes, these are my minions. The new vampires that I have created to help me kill each of you one by one." Eric replied. "I was going to enjoy killing all of you with my brother and my sister, but you all killed them before we had the chance.

"It wouldn't have happened if you all didn't try to kill us first." Alyssa said. In that moment Eric tried to move toward Alyssa as if he was going to hurt her but then something strange happened. Eric was being thrown from one side of the room to the other in mid air.

"What the hell?" I said as I tried to figure out what was going on. Alyssa looked as if she was in a trance. "Alyssa?" I said trying to get her attention. I could hear Eric as he began to get frustrated as he was being thrown around the room. He was cursing as he hit the walls.

"Alyssa!" Amelia yelled. Suddenly everything stopped. Alyssa turned to look over at Amelia as if nothing had happened. "What?" Alyssa asked. "How did you do that?" I asked. "Do what?" Alyssa asked. "You just threw Eric around like a sack of potatoes." Mason replied. "I guess I've tapped into a new power." Alyssa said.

"Yeah. I would say so." Bell replied. Eric started to look angry as he got up off of the floor. "Now that wasn't so nice. I'm going to kill you slow so you can feel every agonizing bit of pain as your life slowly fades away in my hands." Eric said. "Kill them all!" Eric yelled.

As the newborns started to press their attack on us Eric made his way toward Alyssa once again. As Mason tried to move forward to protect her Eric grabbed Mason by his throat and threw him across the room. Alyssa was crouched and ready to defend herself as Eric started to come toward her.

I jumped over Alyssa and pushed Eric back toward the wall as I held on to his black robes. Mason ran over and started to help Alyssa as two of the newborns began to attack her. Caleb and his brothers were fighting another group of newborns while Astarte and his family helped Raven and Bell fight the rest as Benjamin, Shane, and Mary came to my aid.

As I took the dagger of Zan out of my pocket and raised it to Eric's throat he pushed me back across the floor causing the dagger to fly out of my hands. Afterward Eric kicked me so hard that I fell backward and slid across the floor. I slid across the floor so hard that the floor began to come apart. There was now a big gaping whole in the middle of the floor in the tower.

"Mary grabbed the dagger and ran toward Eric. As Mary tried to pierce the dagger through Eric's throat in hopes of decapitating him Eric snatched the dagger out of Mary's hand and punched her in the face. "Mom!" Shane yelled. As Shane ran toward Eric to try and take him out Eric started to move swords off of the wall with his mind.

Eric started to throw them at Shane. As Shane kept running toward Eric and trying to dodge the swords that were flying through mid air Bradley flashed over behind Eric and snatched the dagger out of his hand and stabbed Eric in the neck.

Eric hit Bradley across the face causing him to fly across the room near Mary. As I got the strength to get up off of the floor I saw Eric pull the dagger out of his neck and throw it on the floor by the chair. I knew that if I could just get over to that chair and get the dagger that I could cut off Eric's head and this would all be over.

I just needed a distraction. Suddenly I saw Alyssa nod as if she knew what I was thinking. "Go for it. I'll distract him." Alyssa said. As I made my way across the room Alyssa began to run toward Eric.

I could hear the screams of the newborn vampires as Caleb and the others were helping the Brotherhood kill off these psychotic animals. I took a lot of comfort from that thought as I flashed across the room to make my way over to the dagger.

Alyssa jumped in the air and landed on top of Eric's back. She opened her mouth and pulled Eric's neck forward as she sank her teeth into him. I could hear Eric screaming out from the pain. He was in complete agony.

"Get off me!" Eric sreamed. "Not a chance in hell!" Alyssa screamed back as she sank her teeth into Eric's neck again. Eric flashed out of Alyssa's hands. As Alyssa landed on her feet Eric knocked her to the side. I picked up the dagger and held it at my side as I ran toward Eric.

Before I could use the dagger Eric hit me across the face. I kept the dagger in my grasp as I leaned over toward the chair as I was getting ready to make my move. "It's a shame I have to kill you. I could have used someone like you with your strength and speed." Eric said as he walked up the steps getting ready to kill me.

"What can I say? I learned from the best." I replied as I looked over at Caleb who was about to attack Eric from behind. I shook my head letting Caleb know that I had a plan. Caleb stepped back and looked at the others as he held his hand up as if to tell them to wait.

Bell and Amelia definitely knew what I was doing. "You and your sister are so gifted. I really could have used the two of you. We could have been unstoppable together. We could have taken over this world one city at a time." Eric continued.

"I would rather die." I replied. "You have so much pride don't you?" Eric asked. "Its not just pride. Its common sense and a good heart even though my heart no longer beats." Eric looked as if he was amused by my answer.

"Tell your father hi for me when you meet him in the underworld." Eric said as he lifted his hand up to strike. "Get away from my daughter!" Mary yelled as she ran up toward us. Before Mary could get her hands on Eric I stuck the dagger through his heart. As Eric fell to his knees I took the dagger and cut through his throat making it to where his head would fall off.

As Eric's head fell to the floor along with his body I saw Mary look at me with tears of blood running down her face. "Are you alright?" I asked. "Yeah. I just thought that I would be too late." Mary replied as she wiped the tears of blood off of her face.

"Well you weren't. It's all over now so lets get out of here." I told her. I grabbed a torch off of the wall and threw it on top of Eric's body. Victor and Mason grabbed a torch and lit the newborns up one by one so that they would burn into a pile of ash.

Caleb and Darren grabbed a torch to lead the way as Mary and I followed them. Mason and Victor followed us shortly after. When we got to the end of the stairs we didn't see Pandora and the others waiting for us.

"Where are the others?" I asked. "Their obviously outside." Astarte replied. As we walked outside I saw the children standing next to Pandora as she helped Shane hold Ashley up. "What's wrong?" I asked as I ran over toward them.

"Ashley's in labor!" Shane replied in panicked voice. Mary and Bradley ran over to help. "We need to get her to a place where she can have the baby." I told them. "There's a place not far from here. I'll lead you to it." Mary replied.

We started walking through the woods as Mary led us to a place for Ashley to have her baby. Shane and I walked beside Ashley holding her by the arm on each side to keep her from falling.

As we walked through the woods I could hear the pain in Ashley's voice as she cried out from the labor pains. "Its going to be ok Ashley. Everything is going to be ok." I told her. "Ohhhh!" Ashley cried out. "Be patient Ashley. We're almost there." Mary said. "We need to hurry mother! Ashley is in a lot of pain!" Shane said as he started to panic again.

"We're almost there! Just calm down!" Mary replied. Suddenly we were walking through some bushes. As we came out I saw a little wooden cabin. This is where Bradley brought me after he changed me." Mary said. As we walked inside I felt a sudden feeling of joy. My best friend was about to bring life into the world. It may have been a type of supernatural life but to me it was still a life. I couldn't be more happy for her. This was her moment and my greatest joy.

Chapter 23

The Birth Of New Life

As we got inside the cabin Shane and Mary took Ashley inside the bedroom. The others and I stood in the living room. We were full of joy. "Elizabeth!" Mary yelled. "Yeah?!" I yelled as I stood there in the living room with the others feeling nervous. "Get me some hot water and some rags. The rags are in the drawer in the kitchen and there's a pot setting on the counter." Mary said. "Oh!" Ashley yelled. "Raven!" Ashley yelled. Raven ran toward the bedroom to Ashley's side. "What is it honey?" Raven asked. "Hold my hand. Please!" Ashley said as she felt another pain.

"Its going to be ok Ashley. You can do this." Raven replied as she held Ashley's hand. I'm sorry if I grip your hand too hard. I'm in so much pain." Ashley said. Raven began to laugh. "Are you kidding me? I'm a vampire honey. It would take a lot for you to hurt me beings your still human." Raven replied as she continued to laugh.

"I'll remember that when I'm a vampire soon." Ashley said with a slight smile on her face. "Oh! The baby is coming!" Ashley yelled. "Push her dress up! I've got to deliver this baby quick!" Mary yelled.

"Breathe baby breathe." Shane said as he knelt down beside Ashley to hold her hand while Raven was on the other side. "Elizabeth!"

Ashley yelled. "I'm coming!" I yelled as I ran inside the bedroom holding the pot in my hands with the rags over my shoulder. "Oh!" Ashley screamed. "Your doing good honey." Shane said. "Shut up!" Ashley yelled. "Yes dear." Shane replied. "Don't speak!" Ashley yelled. Shane shook his head as he kept holding Ashley's hand.

"Just do what she says." Raven said with a slight smile as she tried not to laugh. "I see the head!" Mary said. "Oh my god." Darren said shaking his head as if he didn't care to hear that information. "That's child birth honey." Amelia said as she put her hand on Darren's shoulder.

"Don't remind me." Darren replied. Amelia began to laugh. "Ok Ashley one more push!" Mary said. "Ahh!" With in a minute I heard the cries of a newborn child. A hybrid child. Then I smelled blood. Lots of blood.

I began to speak to keep Mary and Shane distracted as well as the others from the blood. "My baby." Ashley said as she passed out. "Ashley!" Shane yelled. "What's wrong?" Raven asked. "Ashley's losing too much blood! Shane you've got to change her now!" I yelled.

Shane nodded and leaned down to bite Ashley's neck. Ashley was passed out from the pain of giving birth to her baby that she didn't even flinch when Shane bit her. After a moment Shane lifted his head up and cut his wrist with his finger nail and squeezed out the blood.

As Shane's blood dropped into Ashley's mouth she started to change. I stood next to Mary as she held Ashley's baby in her arms. "Hand me that red blanket over on the chair." Mary said.

I reached over and grabbed the blanket. Mary took the blanket and wrapped the baby in it. "He's so beautiful." I said as I looked down at the baby. "I'm going out into the living room to show the others. Stay here with Shane and Raven" Mary said. "Alright."
As Ashley laid there on the bed passed out from the pain I started talking to Shane. "You have a son." I said in an excited voice as I put my hand on Shane's shoulder. "Yeah. I never thought that I would ever have a child." Shane replied. "This is a happy day brother. A new life is born."

"Yeah. I'm happy Elizabeth, but I'm worried about Ashley." Shane said as he held Ashley's hand. "Why?" I asked. "What if something goes wrong during the transformation and she doesn't wake up." Shane said in a worried voice. "It won't. Ashley is going to be ok."

As I stood by Shane waiting for Ashley to wake up everyone was having a fit over the baby. Everyone was falling in love with him. "Oh he is just the most precious little thing." Amelia said as she held the baby in her arms. "Of course he is. He's my grandson." Mary replied as she looked at the baby with a slight smile on her face.

"Rug rat number one." Darren said. "Yeah. Rug rat number two will be coming soon enough." Victor said. "How much longer until we break the news to Elizabeth that she's pregnant?" Caleb asked. "Not much longer." Bell replied. "I want to tell her when we get back home to Scotland." Caleb said. "As you wish." Astarte replied.

"So have Shane and Ashley named the baby yet?" Beth asked. "No, but I think once Ashley wakes up her and Shane will pick out a name for him." Mary replied. After ten minutes Ashley woke up.

"Hey stranger." I said with a grin on my face. Ashley's physical appearance stayed the same. The only difference was that she was pale. "Where's my baby?" Ashley asked. "Mother has him. I'll get her to bring him in." Shane replied as he kissed Ashley's forehead and walked out of the room.

"So have you thought about what your going to name the little guy?" I asked. "Yes. Shane and I decided to name him Anthony Shane Collins." Ashley replied. "Wonderful name." Mary said as she walked into the room holding little Anthony in her arms.

"Would you like to hold your son?" Mary asked. "Yeah." Ashley replied as she held her arms out. As Ashley sat on the bed holding her son in her arms she began to cry. "He is so beautiful. He has dark hair just like you Shane." Ashley said. "He has your eyes." Shane replied as he leaned over to kiss Ashley.

"Look at what we did. He's so perfect." Ashley said as the tears continued to fall down her face. This was the happiest moment that all of us had since we destroyed Julian and his family. This was a happy day. We could all finally walk in the sunlight without being burned alive. My best friend had a beautiful baby boy. What more could you ask for?

Today was a wonderful day. Our battle was over. We had won against a fierce enemy once again. We had won against the forces of evil once more. I walked out of the room to let Shane and Ashley have their moment with Mary and Bradley. As I walked into the living room I hugged Caleb as I leaned forward to kiss him on his sweet lips.

"Today is a wonderful day." I said. "Yes it is." Caleb replied. "How come it didn't take Ashley long to change? Why is her physical appearance still the same other than her being pale now?" I asked.

"Well as you know hybrids are half human and half vampire. When a hybrid turns a human it doesn't take them long to change because their only becoming half vampire. As for us we are different. When we change someone it takes a while for them to change because they are not becoming half vampire. They are becoming full vampire." Caleb replied.

"As for the physical appearance of a hybrid their appearance stays the same other than they become pale." Caleb added. "I understand." I replied. In that moment Ashley and Shane walked out into the living room with Mary and Bradley.

"Mary, will you hold Anthony while Shane and I make our announcement?" Ashley asked. "Sure." Mary replied. "Shane and I have something that we want to tell everyone." Ashley said. "Ashley and I are going to get married." Shane said. "That's wonderful." I replied as I went over to hug them.

"Wonderful." Raven said as she hugged Ashley. "Shane and I were wondering if we could get married in Ireland at your family's castle? Is that ok Astarte?" Ashley asked. "Of course." Astarte replied. "We would be delighted." Pandora said.

"Here we go again." Victor said. "I will call the airline and arrange a flight for all of us to Ireland. Call it a wedding gift, but don't get use to my generosity." Connor said. "We wouldn't dream of it." Ashley replied.

Amelia and I started planning the wedding along with Raven, Bell, and Alyssa on our plane ride to Ireland. We were going to throw one hell of a wedding that Ashley and Shane would never forget for centuries to come. This was going to be good.

Between the others and I we would have quite the wedding party that would be remembered throughout eons of time. I was happy to be planning my best friend's wedding. I know I wasn't the most welcoming in the beginning of Ashley becoming one of us, but I just wanted her to be able to have a chance at a happy life.

I do have to admit though that now I am kind of glad that she is one of us. Well atleast half of one of us. It will be nice to have my best friend around. When I think about all of those years that we spent apart because I was vampire I would have to say that it honestly sucked not having her in my life.

Ashley was always a good friend to me and she always will be. I can't wait until we get back to Ireland. This wedding is going to be the best one yet.

Chapter 24

A Ceremony

As soon as we all got to Astarte's castle Amelia and I took Ashley to one of the guest rooms to get her ready for her wedding. Alyssa, Raven, and Bell followed us to get ready as well. Mary and Bradley watched little Anthony while Caleb, Darren, and Victor took Shane into the guest room across the hall to get him ready for the wedding as well. Astarte and his family got prepared and went outside into the garden to wait for us to come out. Benjamin of course was standing outside with them. He was going to do the ceremony since he was after all a priest in his human life.

"I'll get the dress. Elizabeth do something with Ashley's hair and Alyssa do Ashley's make up." Amelia said. "I'll get a nice necklace to go with the dress." Bell said. "I have some nice pins that we can put in Ashley's hair." Raven replied. With the way we were all running around trying to get Ashley ready for her wedding we looked like we were running a vampire salon.

"Here's the dress." Amelia said. The dress was long with thin straps. It was white with a pink ribbon tied around the waist. "Oh Amelia! Its beautiful!" Ashley replied in a happy voice as she hugged Amelia.

As I started to curl Ashley's long and beautiful blonde hair Raven showed Ashley the hair pins. "Oh Raven! These are so pretty." Ashley said. "I knew you would like them." Raven replied as she started putting the pins into Ashley's hair. The pins were white with pink diamonds on them. "My mother passed these on to me when I was eighteen." Raven added. "Oh Raven I couldn't possibly."

"Yes you can." Raven said cutting Ashley off. "Think of this as your something borrowed." Raven added. "Thank you." Ashley replied as she hugged Raven. "Ok the hair is done so now all we need is Alyssa to do her magic on Ashley's make up." I said. "Here's the necklace." Bell said as she walked into room.

"Rosemary said that you could borrow it for the wedding." Bell added. "I thought I was only suppose to have one thing that was borrowed?" Ashley asked. "Well I guess traditions change." Bell replied with a slight smile. "Its beautiful." Ashley said.

The necklace was gold with a pink diamond heart. Alyssa put some white glittery eye liner on Ashley's eyes with some mascara. Bell and Raven had already changed into their dresses so now Amelia and I needed to change.

Bell wore a short dark emerald green dress with a gold ribbon around the waist and Raven wore a long red dress with a black ribbon around the waist. Amelia decided to wear a long thin strapped navy blue dress while I wore a long short sleeved white dress.

"Are we ready?" I asked. "Yeah." Amelia replied. "Come on Ash. Lets get you married." I said as we walked out of the room. Bell, Raven, Amelia and I would walk out first. We were the bridesmaids. Alyssa was the flower girl.

Shane had Caleb be his best man while Darren and Victor stood with Mason watching on the sife line along with Astarte and his family. Caleb, Darren, and Victor wore black suits while Mason stuck to his buttoned up white dress shirt and jeans.

Rosemary, Beth, and Pandora wore long strapless dresses. Little Sky and Serenity stood next to Pandora wearing their little dresses with ruffles at the bottom with lace trimed around them. They were both white.

Alyssa started to walk outside down the isle in the garden. She tossed the white flowers from her basket as she walked down the isle while Star played the wedding music on the harp. Star was quite the talented musician in our family. Bell, Amelia, and Raven started to walk out behind Alyssa as Star continued to play.

It was time for me to walk down the isle next. We were having the wedding in the garden just right outside of Astarte's castle. We didn't exactly have much time for decoration. As soon as I got down to the end of isle to stand next to Bell and the others Ashley began to walk down the isle. She looked beautiful. This was her day. This was her moment.

Shane looked as if he was in a state of shock. He couldn't take his eyes off of Ashley. Mary smiled as she held little Anthony in her arms as she stood next to Bradley with Astarte and the others on the side line. Benjamin began to speak as Ashley joined Shane in the center of the garden.

The garden was beautiful. There were so many flowers. There was even a huge bird bath in the middle of the garden that had a grey angel made out of stone on top of it.

"We are gathered here today to witness the marriage of Ashley and Shane." Benjamin said. "Ashley, do you take Shane to be your husband through out eternity and beyond?" Benjamin asked. "I do." Ashley replied. "Shane, do you take Ashley to be your wife through out eternity and beyond?" Benjamin asked. "I do." Shane replied. Tears of blood began to run down Ashley's face.

"Then now I pronounce you both husband and wife for eternity." Benjamin said. Shane wiped the tears off of Ashley's face as he leaned in to kiss her on the lips. The boys were whistling while the girls were clapping.

Ashley had finally gotten her happy ending. Her heart was no longer broken from when Justin betrayed her. Ashley wasn't falling apart anymore. Shane was in fact the best thing that had happened to my best friend.

"Welcome to the family." I said as I leaned over and hugged Ashley. "Time to party!" Darren said in an excited voice. That's Darren for you. What can you expect? We all started to dance around in the middle of the garden. Today was a day full of joy. I held little Anthony while Mary and Bradley started to dance. Caleb stood beside me as we enjoyed the celebration.

"Caleb?" I said. "Yes love?" Caleb replied. "I want to go home." Caleb looked at me confused. "Home?" Caleb said looking confused. "Yeah. I want to go back to Pensacola for a while. I miss it. Even more I miss being able to go and talk to mom."

Caleb looked as if he understood how I felt. "If you want to go back to Pensacola for a while I don't see why the others would object." Caleb replied. "Are you ok with going back for a while?" I asked. "Of course. We can stay there for a while and then we can go back to Scotland. We can move around."

"Thank you. I love you." I said as I leaned over to kiss Caleb on his soft sweet lips. "I love you too babe." As I looked over at everyone as they were dancing and enjoying the celebration I saw Amelia looking at me as if she knew what I was thinking. She looked at me with a smile as if to say that she approved of my decision to go back to Pensacola for a while.

As I smiled back at her I saw Ashley dancing with Bradley as Mary danced with Shane. Everyone was enjoying themselves. After a moment Mary and Bradley walked over toward us. "Alright Elizabeth its your turn." Bradley said. "You and Caleb can go dance and have some fun while Bradley and I watch little Anthony." Mary said. "Ok." I replied as I gave little Anthony back to Mary.

"Come on babe. Its time for us to dance and enjoy ourselves." Caleb said. I smiled as Caleb grabbed my hand and pulled me toward him as we walked out into the middle of the garden to dance. Everyone was smiling and having such a great time.

It had been long time since I had experienced a moment of true happiness. I was having such a good time that I didn't even think about any of the bad things that I had went through up until this moment.

It was as if nothing else mattered right now except this wonderful day that was full of joy. As I danced with Caleb I felt kind like I did on our wedding day. I felt happy and relieved. I felt excited and hyper. I could bounce off of the walls right now if we had any. I couldn't wait to get home. I wanted to see the city of Pensacola again. I wanted to see my home.

I missed my home so much. I put the thoughts about missing home out of my mind and continued to enjoy the celebration. I would be home again soon enough. For now I would just enjoy where I was at. I would enjoy the moment.

After the celebration was over I stood outside of the castle with my family to said goodbye to Astarte and the others. I hated having to say goodbye to them once again. I was going to miss them so much.

Especially Astarte and Pandora. They may have been vampires but they were definitely the kind of people that you would want to be your parents. I know that's weird to say because their immortal and close to my age but its true. "We have enjoyed spending time with you and your family Caleb." Astarte said.

"The feeling is mutual." Caleb replied. "We hope that you will all come and visit us again soon." Pandora said. "We definitely will." Alyssa replied. "Maybe your visit will be under different circumstances." Connor teased. "Hopefully." I said with a slight smile.

"Come on everyone. You all know how much I love flying first class." Caleb said as he turned and began to walk away. "I guess you all will be leaving now as well." I said as I looked at Raven and Bell. Well actually Benjamin and I have been talking about staying with you and your family." Bell replied. "Really?" I said as I looked at Bell with a shocked face. "Yes." Benjamin replied. "Sky and I would like to stay too." Raven said.

"That's great!" Ashley replied in an excited voice as she leaned over to hug Raven while Shane held little Anthony. "Goodbye." I said as I turned around and walked with the others towards the woods. "Goodbye." Astarte replied. With in a few seconds my family and I were gone. We took off through the woods. "I'm going to miss them." I said. "We all will." Amelia replied.

"What made you all decide to stay with us?" I asked as I looked over at Bell and Raven. "Its just so much fun hanging out with all of you. There's never a dull moment." Benjamin replied as he started to smile.

"I've grown quite fond of you Elizabeth. Your like a sister to me and I don't want to lose that." Bell said. "My reason is a little different." Raven said. "What's your reason?" Ashley asked. "I've always felt close to Caleb and Elizabeth as well as the rest of the family but Ashley when I met you I felt like I could connect with you more than I could with anyone else." Raven replied.

"Oh Raven. Your so sweet." Ashley said as she leaned over to hug Raven. "It may be sweet but it's the truth." Raven replied. "Shane?" I said as I walked toward him. "Yeah?" Shane said as he looked down at little Anthony. "Are you and Ashley leaving with Mary and Bradley or do you plan to stay with us?" I asked.
"I want to stay and be with Elizabeth." Ashley said as she looked over at Shane. Shane began to smile. "So do I." Shane replied. "After all I do need to get to know my sister so she can baby sit." Shane teased.

"Funny." I replied "If you weren't holding little Anthony I'd punch you in your arm." I added. Everyone started to laugh. "Bradley and I would like to stay too." Mary said. "Of course." I replied. "I would like to get to know my mother." I added. Mary looked as if she was about to cry.

Everyone looked as if they were happy that Mary and I were starting to get along. Especially Caleb. "I would like that. Daughter." Mary said as she leaned over to hug me. "There's something that I need to tell everyone." I said as I stopped walking and turned around to face them.

"I know that we have to move around a lot because of what we are but I would like to go back home to Pensacola for a while. Its my home and I miss it but more importantly I think that Alyssa and I should go back so we can stay there for a while and get our closure. I want to make peace with my mother and everthing that happened and the only way that I can do that is to go back there."

"I agree." Alyssa replied. "That's fine with me." Mason said. "Now that we can walk in the sunlight I wouldn't mind hitting the beach."

Darren said. "Only Darren would say that." I replied as I looked over at Caleb. "What?" Darren said as he looked over at Amelia who was shaking her head.

"You are truly one of a kind husband of mine." Amelia replied as she kissed Darren's cheek. "I think it's a good idea." Star said. "Maybe we can lay out in the sun and get a tan." Alyssa said.
"That's a nice thought but it won't happen because our bodies are eternal. How we were when we changed is how we will always be." Caleb replied. "Damn! I'm doomed to spend my eternity without a good tan." Alyssa said as she crossed her arms. We all started to laugh.

"Being a vampire really sucks." Amelia said as she put her arm around Alyssa and smiled. "Funny." Alyssa replied. "Well I guess I better call the airline and make our flight arrangements." Caleb said. "Alright." I replied. "We should have a homecoming party when we get back home." Alyssa said.

"I don't know. I think once we get home I'm just going to relax and enjoy the moment. I'm really tired." I replied. "Are you feeling ok?" Alyssa asked. "Yeah. I'm just tired." I couldn't wait to get back home to Pensacola.

I missed it so much. I knew that I needed to get back and make peace with my past. It was time to move on. It was time to leave all of the bad things in the past and move on to the good. It was time for me to go home.

Chapter 25

Going Home

As I sat on the plane next to Caleb I started to feel a little uneasy in my stomach. Something was wrong. I knew that I shouldn't be feeling like this. I'm a vampire. Vampires don't get sick. At least not like this. Bell and Amelia looked over at me with a slight grin on their faces. Why do they keep doing that? I thought. "What's wrong?" Caleb asked. "I don't feel so good. I feel a little uneasy in my stomach." I replied. "Oh boy." Caleb said as if he knew what was going on.

I thought that I was going to throw up. Luckily for me our plane landed in that moment. I made my way passed everyone on the plane so I could get outside and get some fresh air. "We have got to tell Elizabeth what's going on." Alyssa said as she walked up behind Bell.

"Caleb is going to tell Elizabeth the news when we get home." Bell replied. "I can't wait to see her face." Alyssa said as she began to smile her devious grin. "Me either." Amelia said as she started to laugh she walked up behind us.

"It will be quite a moment." Bell said. "I wish I could see everything like you." Alyssa replied. "Its not always good to see the future ahead of time trust me." Bell said. "Well with everything that happens in this family I would have to agree." Amelia replied. As soon as I got off of the plane I ran over by the gate. After standing by the gate for a minute I started to feel dizzy.

Alyssa came up behind me and caught me as I started to fall over. "Wow!" Alyssa said as she held me in her arms. "Are you ok?" Caleb asked as he walked up behind me. "I don't know. There's something wrong. I know it." I replied

"Lets get you home." Alyssa said. As we walked through the city of Pensacola everything still looked the same. I was happy to be back home. I had missed it so much.

When we got to the house I was surprised to see that it was still in the same condition that we had left it in. Alyssa held on to me as Caleb opened the door for us. As soon as we were inside the house Alyssa took me into the living room where I could sit down on the couch. "Feeling better?" Caleb asked as he came and sat down beside me. "A little. I just wish that I knew what was going on." I replied.

"Just sit on the couch and lay back." Alyssa said. "Try to be still. It will help." Bell said. "You sound like you know a lot about this sort of thing." I said as I looked over at Bell as I laid back and tried to be still. "I do." Bell replied. In that moment everyone looked at Bell as if they were surprised by her words. It was weird.

"Caleb? Amelia? Can I talk to you in the kitchen?" Alyssa asked. "Sure." Amelia replied. "Of course." Caleb said. "What's going on?" I asked. "Oh nothing. I just need to talk to Caleb and Amelia about something." Alyssa replied "Ok." I replied.

"Just relax." Bell said. As I tried to be still and relax Alyssa walked into the kitchen as Caleb and Amelia followed. "What is it?" Caleb asked. "You need to tell my sister that she's pregnant." Alyssa replied. "I am. I just wanted to get her into the house first." Caleb said.

"Elizabeth's symptoms are getting worse. She needs to know that she's pregnant now." Amelia said. "Alright. Let's go tell her." Caleb replied. After a few minutes Alyssa walked out of the kitchen with Caleb and Amelia following behind her.

"Elizabeth there's something that I need to tell you." Caleb said. I sat up and looked at Caleb with worry. I had a feeling that something was wrong. "What's wrong?" I asked. Everyone gathered around as if they knew what Caleb was about to say.

"We haven't been entirely honest with you." Alyssa said. "What are you talking about?" I asked as I began to look worried. "We know what's wrong with you. We know why you've been getting sick a lot lately." Amelia replied. "We just didn't want to tell you until everything had calmed down." Ashley said.

"What's going on?" I asked. Everyone started to smile. Caleb looked as if he was really happy about something. I had no idea what it could possible be but I knew that it wasn't a bad thing with the way that everyone was looking.

I knew it had to be good news. I was hoping that it would be good news. I needed something good in my life right about now.

Chapter 26

A Great Surprise

I sat there on the edge of my seat waiting for Caleb to speak. "Will you tell her already!" Alyssa said as she looked over at Caleb as she began to grow impatient. "Tell me what?" I asked as I started to look worried again. "Elizabeth, there's no easy way to say this but you need to know." Caleb replied. "Need to know what?" I asked. "Your pregnant." Alyssa replied. My mouth fell open as I heard those words. I couldn't believe it. How could I be pregnant? I was a vampire. Vampires can't have children unless its with a human.

"What?" I said as I stood up looking shocked and surprised. "All of the dizzy spells that you have been having as well as the uneasy feeling in your stomach are symptoms of vampire pregnancy." Bell said. "Bell, when you said that you knew what I was going through earlier you meant that you had been pregnant before didn't you?" I asked.

"Yes. I was human when I gave birth to a stillborn baby boy." Bell replied. "Oh Bell." I said as I put my hand over my mouth. "Everything happens for a reason." Bell replied. "How can I be pregnant?" I asked. "There's a prophecy about a vampire that can have children." Benjamin replied.

"When you started getting sick I knew that something was up. I went to my brothers to try and find out what was going on. They told me about the prophecy." Caleb said. "So how long will it be before I have the baby?" I asked. "About two months." Bell replied.

"Two months!" I said as I began to panic. "Don't panic Elizabeth. We will help you through this." Amelia said as she put her hand on my shoulder. "Don't panic! I'm pregnant! I'm a vampire that's pregnant!" Everyone started to smile as if they wanted to laugh. "Oh my god! What do I do?" I said as I began to freak out.

"Well for starters calm down." Ashley replied. "Being pregnant is a wonderful feeling." Ashley added. "Yeah if you like having dizzy spells and an uneasy stomach that makes you feel like your going to puke all the time." I replied as I put my hand on my stomach. Ashley started to laugh. "What goes around comes around." Ashley teased. "You wait until I get over this. I'm going to give you so much---."

"Wow! Man your hostile." Mason said. "You try having a human being I mean a vampire being inside you and then you tell me about hostility." I replied. "Its going to be so nice for the next two months." Darren said as he crossed his arms and shook his head.

"If only you knew." Ashley replied. "Elizabeth there's nothing to worry about. I know that this is sudden and our scared but all of us are going to be right here with you." Bell said.

"I know. I'm sorry if I'm being difficult but I'm just shocked." I replied. "You should have seen Caleb's reaction when Benjamin and I told him." Bell said as she looked over at Caleb and smiled.

"Did he freak out?" I asked. "Oh yeah." Benjamin replied. "He was happy though. Caleb just had a few moments of the normal feelings of fear that follows behind knowing that your going to be a parent." Bell replied.

"You were scared too?" I asked as I looked over at Caleb.

"Yeah I was. I never thought that I would ever have a child. I thought that vampires couldn't reproduce with other vampires but apparently that's not true." Caleb replied. "Its not true for us." Amelia said. "You two are lucky. Elizabeth may be a vampire but she's a blessed one. The rest of us will never know that joy like the two you will." Amelia added.

"Oh Amelia. You will know one day. You may not have a child of your own but you can adopt." I replied. "That is true." Darren said as he smiled over at Amelia. "Yes it is but in order to do that I would have to strip a child of their soul and I don't think that I can do that." Amelia replied.

I felt sorry for Amelia. She would be a great mother. Any child would be blessed to have Amelia's love and kindness. "I know how you feel. If Sky hadn't of been dying when I found her I wouldn't have turned her." Raven said. "I can't believe it. I'm going to have a baby." I said as I started to cry.

Amelia started to cry along with me. She came over and put her arm around me. "You deserve it Elizabeth. Your going to be a great mother." Amelia said. "Thanks Amelia. You're the best." I replied. "I'm planning the baby shower." Alyssa said. "I'm helping." Ashley said. "Here we go." Darren replied as he put his hand on Shane's shoulder.

"We need to have one for Ashley too. We didn't get to throw her one." Alyssa said. "I agree. We should definitely have a baby shower for both of them." Star replied. "Why don't we plan the shower for the two of you." Bell suggested. Ashley and I looked at each other.

"Ok." I replied. "Fine with me." Ashley said. "You can relax and Ashley can spend time with little Anthony and we can plan it all." Amelia said. "Sounds good to me." Ashley replied. "Lets do it." I said.

We all sat in the living room hanging out and talking about my baby and Ashley's baby. Amelia and Bell were going over the baby shower plans with Raven. It was like the perfect family moment. Mary and I talked a lot and began to form a good relationship with each other.

This was one of the best moments of my life. I had everything that I could possibly want. What more could I possibly ask for? I had a beautiful nephew. I had the best husband and family in the world but most of all I was pregnant.

I was carrying a life inside of me. A supernatural life. This was the best thing that had happened to me since I married Caleb. All of the fighting was finally over. All of the vampires who were a threat to our family were finally destroyed. My family and I could finally live in peace.

This was the best thing ever. We could finally live our lives in peace. Everything that we had done up to this moment was worth everything that we went through. I still wish that mom was here but Mary isn't so bad. She is my real mom.

Maybe this is how things are supposed to be. Maybe my life was predetermined before I was born. Who know? Maybe I was meant for this life as well as to go through hard times that came with it.

Life is pretty good now. I want this moment to last forever.

The End.

The Characters

1. Elizabeth Cromwell.
2. Alyssa Cromwell.
3. Caleb Macbeth.
4. Darren Macbeth.
5. Amelia Macbeth.
6. Victor Macbeth.
7. Star Macbeth.
8. Ashley Phillips.
9. Mason Hayes.
10. Raven.
11. Sky.
12. Bell.
13. Benjamin.
14. Astarte.
15. Pandora.
16. Serenity.
17. Rosemary.
18. Connor.
19. Beth.
20. Philip.
21. Mary Collins.
22. Shane Collins.
23. Bradley Collins.
24. Julian.
25. Melina.
26. Eric.
27. Lex.
28. Athena.
29. Eve.
30. William.
31. Joseph.
32. The Medics.
33. Olivia.
34. The Oracle.
35. Isis.
36. Brigit.
37. Braxus.
38. Cyrus.
39. Larva.
40. Anthony Shane Collins.

I would like to thank everyone that has supported me.
Your support means the world to me. Thank you so much.

August Alexander

www.ingramcontent.com/pod-product-compliance
Lightning Source LLC
Chambersburg PA
CBHW032232050726
47591CB00001B/363